AKBAR–THE GREAT MUGHAL

His New Policy and His New Religion

AKBAR–THE GREAT MUGHAL

His New Policy and His New Religion

Ahmad Bashir

Akbar: The Great Mughal
Ahmad Bashir

First Published 1967
First Indian Edition 2009
Reprinted 2025

ISBN 978-81-89833-81-7

Published by
AAKAR BOOKS
28 E Pocket IV, Mayur Vihar Phase I
Delhi 110 091, India
www.aakarbooks.com

Printed at
D.K. Fine Art Press, Delhi

To
Zubaida, Hafiz and Kazi
my mother, father and teacher who love me more than all others I dedicate this humble contribution towards understanding an epoch-making period in our history in the sub-continent of Pakistan and India.

Bashir

Kazi	:	Allama I.I. Kazia (Allama Imdad Ali Imam Ali Kazi), b.1886, son of Kazi Imam Ali Ansari, Rais of Hyderabad, son of Kazi Muhammad Alim Ansari of Batir (Pat), District Dadu.
Hafiz	:	Haji Hafiz-bakhsh, b.1893, son of Ilahi-bakhsh, son of Haji Allah-bakhsh *alias* Haji Bakha of Firozpur, son of Mian Rahmat, son of Mian Ahmad of Kasur.
Zubaida	:	Subaida Begum, b.1899, daughter of Abd-ul-Majid, son of Karim-bakhsh of Firozpur, son of Muhammad Yusuf, son of Hafiz Ghulam Husain of Kasur.

Contents

Talking of Ahmad Bashir's Book

In many ways, Ahmad Bashir's book arouses great interest. That it was written by a Pakistani historian in the 1960s tells us a great deal about the liberal intellectual milieu then prevalent in the newly created nation. In that milieu historians like I.H. Qureshi and Moinul Haq were seeking legitimacy for the creation of Pakistan in medieval history and blaming emperor Akbar for the fall of Mughal Empire who, according to them had diluted the purity of Islam by inducing an interface between it and other religions, especially Hinduism – all denounced as *kufr*. Clearly Islam was the single entry point for them in all their endeavours at historical studies and the Mughal empire was a *Muslim* empire per se. If one needed to bend history to this end, so be it. Ahmad Bashir too sought his entry into the subject through Islam, or, more broadly, religion in general. One can sense an interesting, almost palpable tension in his work, tension between his loyalty to Islam and loyalty to the discipline of history, where evidence is treated as the supreme arbiter. In the end he yields to the discipline at every crucial moment. In that important sense, Bashir's is a rebellious book, a challenge to the sort of history the state was patronising and its official historians were hurriedly writing. Again and again he is led by his evidence to be 'fair' to Akbar and give him credit for being 'great'.

It is also significant that he chose to italicise the Hindu names that occur in the book. Perhaps unknowingly, he was precociously highlighting the cultural loss of his society where Hindu names needed to be highlighted in order to be recognised. The Indian publisher has fortunately retained the italics as in the original version.

V.A. Smith had, way back in 1917 in his *Akbar the Great*

Mogul, 1542-1605, published from Oxford, called Abu'l Fazl, Akbar's courtier and historian 'a shameless flatterer' and Ahmad Bashir has repeated that damning observation with approval. That is a pity, for it demonstrates the modern historians' failure to look beyond the surface where Abu'l Fazl was seeking to construct an alternative teleology of history, disengaging it from the axis of Islam and transforming it into part of universal history where Akbar's 'divinity' raised him above denominational identities. Akbar was, for Abu'l Fazl, not a 'Muslim' ruler but the ruler of all his subjects. Even so, Bashir uses Abu'l Fazl's testimony extensively, almost on every page and usually quite fairly.

One special feature of the book is the enumeration of all the Hindu names with a link with Akbar in one list or another. This book should be of help to students who need the information for their own study, instead of having to look out in numerous scattered sources.

I greatly enjoyed reading the book and I am very happy that Aakar Books, have decided to publish it in India almost with a sense of adventure, which is forever their forte.

Harbans Mukhia

About the Author

It is one of those ironies of times that a scholar is completely forgotten simply because either his work is not published or goes unnoticed because of lack of publicity. Professor Ahmad Bashir was one such author whose works were never properly published and reviewed. I knew him as a student and later as a colleague at the University of Sindh where he was Professor and Head of the Department of History. Before that he had served as Associate Professor at the University of Karachi.

Professor Bashir was a wonderful teacher. His special field of interest was medieval India but he had wide interests in English, Urdu and Persian literatures as well; and he was a good art critic too. His only interests in life were collecting books, acquiring knowledge and then passing it on to his students. He spent a large part of his salary in purchasing books and never thought of having a house built for himself. He led a simple life and was honest—a man of integrity who never deviated from his principles.

There is a sad story about his book on Akbar, his doctoral thesis that he had wanted to publish at his own expense. The University printing press started work on it in 1963 and took nearly seven years to complete it. The reason was that Prof. Bashir was not satisfied sometimes with the typeface and sometimes with the quality of the paper. He was a perfectionist and very minutely did his own proof reading. When finally the book was printed, he reserved 50 copies for his friends. He negotiated with several parties for the rest of the copies but refused to give them to the booksellers on their own terms. The result was that the volumes remained packed in boxes and were wasted because of worms and humidity. Save for those 50 copies the rest of the books never saw the light of the day.

His other writings also remained mainly unread. He wrote a *History of Kusur,* his home town. He corrected the manuscript and rewrote it several times. Sadly, there remains no trace of it following Professor Bashir's death. When he was at the University of Sindh, we had founded a writers' club which used to gather every Wednesday. There he presented his novelette entitled *Bijan Tawaif* (Bijan, the Courtesan), devoted to the final days of Wajid Ali Shah's Lucknow. This book too remained unpublished.

I met Professor Bashir for the last time in Kusur in 1988 and found him in a miserable state, facing huge financial problems. He told me that after his retirement he had spent seven years alone in a room with his books. In Kusur he had no company and during his last days he also lost his eyesight—a great handicap for anybody but more so for a scholar. He died in 1991.

I hope reprinting this book will restore Professor Bashir's scholarly reputation at least in the academic world. I, as his student, am thankful to Aakar Books for undertaking this publication.

May 18, 2008
Lahore

Mubarak Ali
Former Professor
Dept of History, Sindh University
Karachi
and Former Director
Goethe Institute, Lahore

Preface

To write about Akbar's work is to invite argument, yet the spirit of enquiry cannot be thus silenced. Here is one more exposition of his beliefs and achievements.

I have based my conclusions entirely upon important contemporary sources. When they existed, I could not see the wisdom of using later works based upon them. Moreover, these later works are defective in the field in which I have worked. Many of Akbar's acts and terms continued after him, but they lost their original religious significance and it is thus that they are stated in later works. Some of the writers have interpreted the term Chela, the introduction of the Ilahi Era and celebration of the Hindu festivals of Dasahra and Divali on these lines, quoting later works. Contemporary sources do not warrant this. Similarly, to divide the Regulations of Akbar's New Religion and discuss them as 'The Court Ceremonies', 'His Social Reforms' and 'Some of his Administrative Measures' is to compromise the truth. They formed various aspects of Akbar's New Religion.

The most important authority upon Akbar's Religion is Badauni. His language may be defective—the wailing and damming of a mortified soul—but he is usually not far from the truth. Nizam-ud-Din Ahmad is generally reliable in what he writes. Abu-l-Fazl's ponderous volumes of *Akbarnama,* The History of Akbar, with its gigantic Appendix, *Ain-i-Akbari*, The Regulations of Akbar, are indispensable for the student of this period. Day to day events are recorded in detail therein with due regard to chronology; here I have tried to read the language of events rather than of Abu-l-Fazl himself and thus have constructed Chapters I, II and III. His work is a Blue Book in the fullest sense of the term. Wherever Akbar's name is compromised however, Abu-l-Fazl is the least reliable. To read him without the correctives of Nizam-ud-Din Ahmad and Badauni is to get a wrong picture, undertoned and overtoned with many a sable shade completely obliterated. The historical information presented in *Akbarnama* and the scientific statistical method of *Ain* are remarkable, but Heavens dance to the tune of Akbar in the pages of this shameless flatterer, the intellectual giant, the moral wretch.

I have not tried to approach the Jesuit writings on Akbar through translations. They are so full of hearsay that the historians have mostly accepted their statements only where supported by some contemporary authority in Persian. If that has to be the test applied, to quote and refer to them seemed to me simply decorating my pages with iverted commas and adding to the diversity of references in the footnotes.

Chapter I gives an outline of the work of Akbar in building his new polity for Muslims and Hindus, and brings out various aspects of its inner working. Before passing to Chapter II the reader will gain from Appendix A a fuller impression of the religious beliefs and practices of Akbar during the period when he introduced the measures which built his new polity and gave rise to a new cultural pattern. In his endeavour to present Akbar as 'a man not really interested in the tombs of saints' even at this time, Abu-l-Fazl has made him out a hypocrite. In this matter I have followed Badauni and Nizam-ud-Din Ahmad. Chapter II deals with the change of Akbar's ideas and the influence on him of Shaikh Mubarak and Abu-l-Fazl. They are generally believed to have been responsible for Akbar's Din-i-Ilahi. This chapter shows how different was their plan. Chapter III leads us to the consequences of the Neo-Islamic regime. Chapter IV brings us to the climax or the anti-climax of our story—the New Religion of Akbar. The various Regulations of this religion were issued at different times. To give a complete picture of its every aspect, I have put all the regulations concerning an aspect, together. The dates in the margin may help the reader, however, to find out their exact sequence. For the same reason I have added the regulations and beliefs already discussed in the preceding chapter, although it has involved some repetition.

At the end of the book the reader will not find a Verdict on Akbar : how many units of Islam were in him and how many units of other religions. I have simply placed the facts, as recorded in contemporary sources, before the reader. The interested reader may himself work out this simple arithmetic if he believes in the disintegration of a personality. I have studied Akbar as a man and as a ruler and found him to be a great man and a great ruler.

This research work was done at the London University under the supervision of Professor C.H. Philips. He took personal interest in the topic. I am thankful to him for his valuable guidance.

Ahmad Bashir

The Emperor

HIS NEW POLITY

Chapter I

Akbar : His Achievement

Many events come about accidentally and often it is only afterwards that principles relating to them are evolved. A man of affairs sometimes may take an unrelated action and if the outcome proves helpful, a certain policy is seen to emerge. But when the line of action of a responsible man is discussed, it is often taken for granted that he was following from the very beginning a considered policy. Action in life springs so often from feelings rather than thought and meditation. But all too often the achievements of great men are attributed to their unusual reasoning powers. Besides, the imagination of writers plays wonders with some historical figures. Henry V remains what Shakespeare has made of him. Harun-ur-Rashid always moves in the romance of the Arabian Nights. All this has happened in the case of Akbar, the 'Great Mogul'.

In popular imagination he lives as one who tried to unite all his subjects by promulgating a common religion and by marrying many Rajput princesses. Even thoughtful writers have dubbed his marriage with the first Rajput princess, when he was only nineteen, as 'a proof manifest to all the world that Akbar had decided to be the Padshah of his whole people—Hindus as well as Mohammadans',[1] and have regarded it as the fruit of his thinking,[2] which secured for him the powerful support of her family.[3] But a critical study of contemporary sources reveals rather a different story.

In 1554, the year before Akbar came to the throne, Majnun Khan Qaqshal was in charge of the fort of Narnaul. It was attacked by Haji Khan, a general of Sher Shah, and his ally was Raja Bhar Mal Kachhwaha, ruler of Amber. They besieged the fort and the garrison were in a miserable plight. The Raja interceded and a settlement was patched up. The fort was taken, but Majnun Khan was allowed to leave unmolested.[4]

After the battle of Panipat, when Akbar was at Delhi, Majnun Khan talked of the good offices of Bhar Mal. Akbar liked the turn he had done and called him to his court. Bhar Mal, with his sons and relatives, reached Delhi and was well received. The veteran Rajput general for the first time met the boy emperor of thirteen. It seems the youth was impressed by the general's fatherly love and he, in turn, by the young man's promising youth. The Raja and his relatives were given the robes of honour and Akbar personally saw them off. He was on a ferocious elephant at the moment and the beast was dashing this way and that. Whichever dirction the brute turned, people ran away in fright. But when it rushed towards the Raja and his companions, they remained where they were, unperturbed. Akbar appreciated this display of courage[5] and when he was bidding farewell to the Raja, he added, 'We shall enrich you very much'.[6]

Akbar married his sister, Bakhshi Banu Begum, to Mirza Sharf-ud-Din Husain in 1560 and Ajmer, Narnaul and the surrounding country were given in his jagir. The Mirza prepared to attack Amber, the capital of Bhar Mal. Meanwhile, Suja, a claimant to the Raja's throne, son of Puran Mal, the elder brother of Bhar Mal, had joined him. The Mirza led his forces against Amber. He could not dislodge the Rajputs completely, but forced the Raja to sign a humiliating treaty, by which he was to pay a tribute and his son, Jagan Nath, and two of his nephews, Raj Singh and Khankar,[7] were taken as hostages.

In 1561 the Mirza had determined to organize large forces and annihilate the Kachhwahas. Akbar was on pilgrimage to the tomb of Khwaja Muin-ud-Din Chishti at Ajmer, when, at Kalavali, Chughtai Khan informed him of the maltreatment Bhar Mal had received at the hands of Sharf-ud-Din Husain; he had been forced to leave his capital long since and the Mirza was preparing to launch a new attack on Amber. Akbar at once despatched him to bring the Raja to the court. At Deosa Bhar Mal's brother, Rupsi and Rupsi's son, Jai Mal, came to pay their homage to the emperor. Next day Chughtai Khan escorted to the court Bhar Mal and his relatives and chieftains at Sanganir. Akbar treated them with kindness, appreciated their loyalty and showed them marks of favour.[8]

The Raja pondered over the problem of the Kachhwaha relations with the Mughul government. There might be a sympathetic Chughtai Khan, but most of the nobles might not be expected to be unlike Sharf-ud-Din Husain. The most considerate of them all was the Emperor himself. Closer relations with him, therefore, formed the obvious policy. Hence, instead of being a Hindu tributary, he thought of becoming a close relative of the Emperor. To this effect, through some of the most trusted persons round the Emperor, he proposed the marriage of his daughter with him. Akbar accepted his proposal and sent him to prepare for the nuptials. Chughtai Khan was ordered to accompany him.[9]

At Sambhar, when Sharf-ud-Din Husain came to pay his homage and proffer his presents, Akbar, in order to put Bhar Mal perfectly at ease, demanded the hostages from him.[10]

On Akbar's return journey, at Sambhar, Sharf-ud-Din Husain presented Jagan Nath, Raj Singh and Khankar before the Emperor. In the same city was celebrated the famous marriage with the Kachhwaha princess. Near Ranthambhor, Raja Bhar Mal, with all his sons and relatives, reached the royal camp and paid his homage. The Raja said good-bye to his newly-wedded daughter and son-in-law and returned, while his son and grandson, Bhagwan Das and Man Singh, and other relatives accompanied them to Agra. Man Singh had been taken into the Imperial service.[11]

Akbar and the Rajputs

The events speak for themselves. The Raja had fallen on evil days. He was being harassed by the Mughul generals. His son and nephews were in the hands of the enemy as hostages and the himself was seeking refuge among the hills of the desert. His state was not strong enough to withstand the onslaughts of the Mughuls, neither was there any Chitor to provide an asylum for some time. The small principality of Amber was the first in the way of an invader of Rajputana from Agra or Delhi. His predecessor, his elder brother, Raja Puran Mal, was defeated and killed when he opposed Mirza Hindal.[12] He himself had once submitted to Babur and another time to

Humayun. To have peace and security he sought a matrimonial alliance. The kind-hearted Akbar accepted the propsal and the marriage took place. It was not the result of a considered policy on the part of Akbar. It was just a marriage with a Hindu princess, which was not a new thing. Firoz Shah Tughluq was the son of a Hindu princess, daughter of Rana Mal, Raja of Abohar, in the Firozpur district, in the Panjab.[13] Humayun himself had a Hindu wife, daughter of Raja Choka Parhar.[14]

It was not to prove that Akbar had decided to be the emperor of his whole people, Hindus and Muslims, in a different way. Neither was there the question of securing the powerful support of the family of the bride, who were themselves seeking the Emperor's support against Imperial generals. Due to the recent inroads and the expected Mughul invasion, the people of the Amber state were so panic-stricken that when Akbar approached Deosa, the town and the country around were evacuated.[15]

Taking Man Singh into the Imperial service was also not an unheard of innovation. Hindus had been in the Imperial service under various Sultans, even under Mahmud of Ghazna.

If there was any anticipation in the matter, it was on the part of the old man, Raja Bhar Mal. He accepted an overlord to keep intact his state. It was true to the Indian tradition. Rajas would always accept an assertive and more powerful neighbour as their overlord, Maharajadhiraj. Political marriages also were not unknown in India, and seeking a husband for one's daughter was not and is not, considered derogatory to one's self-respect. At the 'Swaimber'[16] not a Prithvi Raj but a Sanjogita selects the consort. In the Indian tradition, the wife is not the prize that a husband wins, but the husband is the prize that a wife wins. Bhar Mal, no doubt, secured a good prize for his daughter.

Bhar Mal made an alliance with the Emperor and other Rajput princes followed suit. Each made a separate alliance of his own. No one thought of organizing a combined opposition. The Rajputs had not outlived the clannish life. Their states were established on the same basis. They would fight against each other. They would fight against an invader individually, but could not get together as an allied force. The two such attempts they ever made, one against Muhammad Ghuri and the other against Babur, failed. The former simply because the injured pride of a Jai Chand would not permit him to join hands with a Prithvi Raj to avoid common ruin. Their clannish pride would not permit them to serve under one another. In the Treaty by which the fort of Ranthambhor was surrendered to Akbar one of the terms was that the chiefs of Bundi would not be put under a Hindu commander.[17]

Moreover, the Sultanate of Delhi had been there for more than three hundred years and to come to terms with a powerful sultan had been the customary policy of Rajput princes. By this time, it was no longer a foreign power, but had become one of the states of the country, playing its part on the common chess-board of politics, whose help was sought by one state against another. For instance, Raja Bhar Mal not being the first son of his father, his nephew, son of his elder brother, had claimed the throne and joined the enemy, Sharf-ud-Din Husain. The Raja, when in trouble from within as well, sought Akbar's help.[18] Similarly, when Chandra Sen of Jodhpur succeeded his father, Rai Maldev, on the throne, his elder brother, Ram Rai, joined the invading Mughuls.[19]

Their clannish animosity was still more pronounced. When the fort of Mirtha was surrendered by Dev Das and he was leaving the place with his 500 Rajput cavalrymen, the people responsible for the destruction of these Rathors were the Kachhwahas in the Mughul army.[20]

To expect from such people, therefore, modern nationalism—something which did not exist at the time—and to accuse Bhar Mal and other Rajput princes of national betrayal is unjust. The various races in India did not consider themselves as one nation. Neither was the whole of India considered as one country. The inhabitants of every state formed a people. Every state was the motherland of her subjects.

The marriage of the Amber princess is one of the happiest events in history. It leavened with love the relations of ruler and the ruled. It gave a different turn to Muslim rule in India. Because the parties contracting a marriage this time proved very different from their predecessors. When a Hindu Raja would resist Muslim arms for long or would rebel again and again and was at last defeated, the hand of his daughter was sometimes demanded as one of the terms of the peace treaty. Her stay in the harem was considered a restraint against her father's future misbehaviour. She was a hostage in a sense. Most of the Hindu-Muslim political marriages before Akbar were of this nature. The sultan would not favour his Hindu queen's father or brothers or trust them as his relatives and make them nobles of his court. On the other hand, the Raja would consider one of his daughters as lost in the combat and was not interested in any way in the fortunes of the dominions of his son-in-law. He was not prepared to come and serve him and make a common cause. The princess was converted to Islam and would lead the life of a Muslim 'malika', without any political consequences. The sultan would exact an annual tribute, if he could do it. The Raja would pay it, if he could not withhold it.

Akbar did not demand the hand of the Rajput princess as a condition of peace. On the other hand, Bhar Mal planned his policy to be of love and service rather than subjection and isolation. He married his daughter to Akbar, loved him as his son-in-law and was prepared to serve him whenever required with his whole Kachhwaha force. To betray the husband of his daughter was out of the question for him.

Akbar valued Rajput co-operation and treated them as his most trusted nobles. Man Singh was taken into the Imperial service and he rose in rank rapidly. The Emperor did not annex any part of their state. They would rather receive extra jagir for the maintenance of the additional corps kept for the Emperor's service.

At the Mathura fair the Government used to collect a tax. The year after his marriage with the Amber princess Akbar happened to be there at the time of the fair and tax-collection. To provide amenity for the Hindus he abolished this tax.[21]

This generous treatment on the part of Akbar could not fail to impress other Rajput princes and helped them to reconsider their relations with the Mughul Emperor. A matrimonial alliance would secure their possessions and ensure for them an extra-ordinary position in the Mughul hierarchy.

In 1570, when Akbar was at Ajmer, Rai Kalyan Mal, Raja of Bikaner, visited him to pay his homage and desired his niece, daughter of his elder brother, Khan,[22] to become an empress. Akbar accepted his proposal and married the Bikaneri princess.[23] Kalyan Mal's son, Rai Singh, later on rose in the Imperial service.

At the same time Akbar was informed that although Raval Har Rai, Raja of Jaisalmer, had not come to pay his homage to the Emperor so far, yet he considered himself as one of his loyal vassals and wished his daughter to become an Imperial queen, and that he wished some noble of the court to be sent to Jaisalmer to escort the princess to the Royal palace. Akbar agreed to this arrangement and the work was entrusted to Raja Bhagwan Das.[24]

A similar propsal was put forward by Raval Askarn, Raja of Dungarpur, in 1576 and the Emperor sent Rai Lunkarn and Raja Birbar to bring to the capital another Rajput consort for him.[25]

A daughter of Rai Maldev of Jodhpur was also given in marriage to Akbar by her brother, Rai Udai Singh.[26]

When Prince Salim was fifteen and Akbar began to think of his marriage, he came to know that Raja Bhagwan Das desired to marry his own daughter to the prince. The Emperor welcomed the proposal and in February, 1584, the marriage of the Imperial crown prince was celebrated with great pomp and show.[27]

Two years later Rai Singh, Raja of Bikaner, desired a similar alliance and Prince Salim was married to his daughter.[28]

The third powerful Royal house of Rajasthan was that of the renowned Rai Maldev of Jodhpur. His son, Rai Udai Singh, too gave in marriage to Prince Salim his daughter, destined to become the mother of Shahjahan.[29]

A daughter (or niece) of Raval Bhim, Raja of Jaisalmer, was also married to Prince Salim.[30]

A grand-daughter of Rai Maldev of Jodhpur, daughter of his son, Rai Mal, was married to Akbar's third son, Prince Danyal.[31]

Besides these princesses of the leading Rajput Royal Houses, some other Hindu ladies were also married into the Royal family. Two more wives of Prince Salim were the daughters of Darya Mal Bhas[32] and Keshav Das Rathor.[33] Another of Danyal's wives was a daughter of Dalpat Ujjainiya.[34]

These Rajas with their Rajput contingents began to help Akbar in building the imposing fabric of the Mughul Empire. They served him with unfaltering loyalty. In the second Gujarat expedition against Muhammad Husain Mirza in 1573, which young Akbar led himself, we find Rajputs fighting for their master with great courage, completely unmindful of their own lives. Akbar was commanding the battle, but he was also fighting among the rank and file. When he personally attacked Muhammad Husain, Bhagwan Das accompanied him. Again he was in front of the Emperor shooting arrows at the enemy when Ikhtiyar-ul-Mulk drew near. Man Singh Darbari, Karn—a grandson of Maldev—and Raghu Das Kachhwaha fought like heroes and the last-named fell on the battlefield. Others who were always around him in this expedition included Jagan Nath, Rai Sal, Jai Mal, Raja Dip Chand, Duvar Bhalla, Har Das, Ram Chand, Sanwal Das, Jagmal Patvar and Ram Das Kachhwaha.[35]

The Management of the Rajputs

But to keep these diverse elements together was not an easy job. Only the master mind of an Akbar could hold them to serve a single purpose. He knew how to feed the pride of these chivalrous clans. In the Gujarat expedition in 1573, when the Mughuls were approaching the enemy and Akbar and his soldiers were donning their armour, he saw Jai Mal, son of Rupsi, a brother of Raja Bhar Mal, wearing a very heavy coat of mail. The kind-hearted Emperor gave him royal armour instead. His coat of mail was given away to Rai Maldev's grandson, Karn, who had nothing to protect his body. Now the clannish feud between the Kachhwahas of Amber and Rathors of Jodhpur was too bitter to allow the ancestral armour of one to fall into the hands of the other. Rupsi, therefore, sent for it from the Emperor. Akbar replied that he had given his son his own fine armour in exchange and that his demand was contrary to the spirit of love and friendship. Rupsi in anguish put off his coat of mail to fight without it. Akbar also took off his armour and remarked, 'Well, if in this battle to fight without armour is set as the test of courage and bravery by our warriors, it won't be chivalrous for us to fight in armour.'[36] This sublime retort eased the situation and the proud Rajput came to tender his apologies, pretending that he had taken 'bhang',[37] which had been the cause of his misdemeanour.[38]

Akbar did not feed their pride only. He would reward and honour his loyal servants.[39] When they began to serve him on the battlefield, he would not collect from them *Jizya*,[40] the tax which the non-muslims in a Muslim state had to pay in lieu of military service, and after sometime he formally abolished it.[41] On his return from Kabul, when he had crossed the Ravi, Raja Bhagwan Das requested a Royal visit. The Emperor granted his wish and honoured him by going to his palace[42] at Lahore. He would also console them in their bereavements. When Govardhan, son of Raja Askarn, brother of Raja Bhar Mal, was murdered, Akbar personally went to Askarn's house for condolence.[43] Man Singh, while Governor of Bengal, was ordered to accompany Prince Salim against Rana Pratap. His son, Jagat Singh, was sent to officiate for him in Bengal. The young man unfortunately died on the way near Agra. To console the bereaved heart of the Raja and the mourning Kachhwahas, Akbar appointed Jagat Singh's son, Maha Singh, to officiate for his grandfather, although he was only a boy at that time.[44]

Akbar expected his nobles also to have regard for Rajput chiefs. On one occasion the nobles were engaged in falconry. The hawk of Rai Sal's son alighted on a tree and Rustam Mirza's retinue got hold of it. Rajputs, men of Rai Sal, reached the spot and a hot dispute ensued, which led to actual fighting. The Mirza hurried there to disengage them and was himself wounded in the attempt. He was able to arrest the impetuous Rajputs at last. But, instead of punishing them himself, he sent them to Rai Sal. When Akbar heard of this forebearance on the part of Rustam Mirza, he praised him.[45]

Moreover, when the Rajputs entered his service, Akbar began to trust them. Confidence begets confidence. When

Khanzaman Ali Quli Khan, the rebel Governor of Jaunpur, crossed the Ganges and thus broke the pledge on which he had been pardoned, Akbar, being still in the vicinity, at once decided to march against him with a light force. Among those few left in charge of the main imperial army was *Raja*[46] *Bhagwan Das.*[47] Similarly, two years later, when Akbar, on march once more against Khanzaman, being suddenly informed about the enemy's movements by his scouts, started at once to fight him with only a handful of soldiers, the main army was to follow him under *Bhagwan Das* and Khwajajahan.[48]

Akbar was on his way to invade Gujarat, in 1572, when the good tidings of the birth of another son at Ajmer was brought to him near Nagaur. He named him Sultan Danyal and the little prince was ordered to be taken to Amber, when one month old, to be brought up under the care of the virtuous *Rani of Raja Bhar Mal.*[49]

In 1573 the Mirzas rebelled in Gujarat. Akbar hurriedly began to prepare for setting forth and sent some of his nobles with their armies in advance at once. The royal harem was to go with them. Among those who were in charge of the harem were *Raja Bhagwan Das* and *Rai Rai Singh* of Bikaner.[50]

When Akbar went on his expedition against Gujarat in 1572, the man in whose hands he left the capital was *Raja Bhar Mal*.[51] When he marched against the Mirzas next year, the capital, with all its treasures, was again entrusted to the same *Old man of Amber.*[52]

Akbar and the Hindus in General

Akbar had not only the services of Rajputs, he had recruited other Hindus also in the Imperial service.

The future Great Emperor from the very beginning had a most imperious nature. The consciousness of his position gave him extra determination to play his role. He was not an inactive tool in the overthrow of Bairam Khan. His surprise march against the misbehaving victorious general in Malwa, his expedition against Khanzaman, the rebellious Governor of Jaunpur, and the treatment he meted out to Adham Khan, his foster-brother, and Khwaja Muazzam, his maternal uncle, made it clear that all had to serve his will. He was to reward them; they were to serve him.

Hindu Rajas had been defeated and had become tributary in the past. But the sultans were content to receive the annual tribute. It was Akbar who wanted them to serve him like his nobles, to come with their contingents and fight the Emperor's battles. Other Hindus, besides the Rajas, were also to serve the Emperor. He desired their assistance in running the administration of the state. With their aid he wanted to subdue the refractory and make further conquests.

It is to this inborn will to rule that we can trace the origin of Akbar's policy of co-operation, rather than, as Sharma says,[53] to his concern to make Hindus interested in not letting his family line on the throne cut short in the distant future like that of Albaris, Khaljis, Tughluqs, Sayyids, Lodis or Suris.[54] He was not old enough at nineteen to indulge in such speculations. He was youthful enough to assert his will. And when those Hindus who entered his service first proved that Hindus could be dependable, he could see the advantages.

Soon after he become independent of Bairam's control Akbar was requiring not only Rajputs but all Hindus to come and serve him. In his perilous fighting against the dacoits in 1562 at Paraunkh he was accompanied by Raja Buddhi Chand and Raja Bhagwan Das.[55] Todal Mal had entered the government service by 1562, as we find him this year sending to the court Raja Ganesh, the defeated hill-chieftain of the Panjab.[56] Next year among those who were sent against the Gakkhars there were two Hindu Rajas of the Panjab, Raja Kapur Dev and Raja Ram Chand.[57] In the ninth year of his reign Akbar was fighting in Malwa against the rebel Governor, Abd-Allah Khan Uzbek, accompanied by Pitr Das and Todar Mal.[58] Next year when Akbar marched against Khanzaman, Todar Mal was one of the two generals sent against Khanzaman's brother, Bahadur Khan. This time there were more than one or two Hindu generals fighting for the Emperor. Besides Todar Mal there were Raja Mitr Sen, Kurmsi, Pitr Das and Rai Sal Darbari.[59]

Thus we find that Akbar was enlisting all Hindus in his service. They had been in the Imperial service previously too.

But they used to be in meagre numbers, most of them holding minor posts in the Revenue Department.[60] Akbar enrolled them without any let or hindrance. And he threw open even the highest posts in the state for them. It was something startling.

When Todar Màl was promoted in the Revenue Department, Muslim nobles waited upon the Emperor and requested him to remove him from his post. Akbar's reply illustrates his attitude: no harm was going to come if able and loyal Hindus were raised to high posts.[61] He remarked, 'Everyone of you has a Hindú in his service. What harm is going to come if we have a Hindu in ours?'[62]

Akbar made all his subjects equally eligible for all posts. He recognised merit. No one suffered from any disability. The government of the country became of Muslims and Hindus alike. They were put on various services together.[63] Hindus were serving under Muslim nobles. Muslims were fighting under Hindu generals. They were all serving the Emperor. Whether their immediate superior was Hindu or Muslim was of no account.[64]

Hindus in Akbar's service rose to the highest ranks in the empire. Man Singh reached the highest rank of the Haft Hazari, the Commandant of Seven thousand cavalry. Todar Mal became Akbar's Diwan, the Finance Minister, next only to the Emperor. Loyal service would not go unrewarded. Salbahan was a musketeer in the Emperor's service. He was made Raja Salbahan.[65]

When a government servant secured the 'mansab' or rank of the commandant of more than five hundred cavalry, he entered the nobility.[66] Akbar's nobles included :

Raja Bhar Mal Panj Hazari[67]
Raja Bhagwan Das Panj Hazari
Raja Man Singh Haft Hazari
Raja Rai Singh Chahar Hazari
Raja Kalyan Mal Do Hazari
Raja Udai Singh Yak Hazar Panj Sadi
Jagan Nath Panj Hazari
Askarn Yak Hazari
Jagmal Yak Hazari

Rupsi Yak Hazar Panj Sadi
Salhadi Haft Sadi
Madhav Singh Sih Hazari
Pratap Singh Yak Hazari
Raj Singh Sih Hazari
Khankar Do Hazari
Jagat Singh Yak Hazar Panj Sadi
Sakat Singh Yak Hazari
Raja Lunkarn Do Hazari
Todar Mal Chahar Hazari
Rai Pitr Das Sih Hazari
Rai Surjan Do Hazari
Rai Bhoj Yak Hazari
Rai Durga Sashodhiya Yak Hazar Panj Sadi
Raja Gopal Do Hazari
Ram Das Kachhwaha Do Hazari
Rai Sal Darbari Do Hazar Panj Sadi
Birbar Do Hazari
Bhao Singh Do Hazari
Maha Singh Do Hazari
Raja Ram Chand Bhughela Do Hazari
Medni Rai Chauhan Yak Hazari
Kalyan Das Yak Hazari
Dharu Haft Sadi
Raja Syam Singh Yak Hazari
Raja Jagman Chauhan Yak Hazari and
Rai-rayan Bikrmajit Panj Hazari.[68]

Besides these 36 Hindu mansabdars in the higher ranks, 29 others are mentioned in the lower, down to the mansab of the Commandant of Two hundred horsemen. Among the Panj Sadi[69] there were Raval Bhim of Jaisalmer, Durjan Singh, Sahal Singh, Dalpat son of Raja Rai Singh of Bikaner, Jagmal Patvar, Parmanand Kshatri, Ram Chand Bundela of Orchha, Raja Mukutman Bhedoria and Raja Ram Chand of Orissa.

The Chahar Sadi were Ram Chand Kachhwaha, Rai Manohar son of Raja Lunkarn and Balka Kachhwaha. The Sih Sadi included Ballabhdhar Rathor, Keshav Das, Tulsi Das Jadun, Man Singh Kachhwaha and Krishn Das. The mansab of Do Sadi was held by Rai Ram Das Diwan, Jagat Singh, Mathura Das Kshatri, Sanwal Das Jadun, Udand of Orissa, Keshav Das Rathor *son of Jai Mal the*[70] *defender of Chitor,* Sundar of Orissa, Suthra Das, Sanga Patvar, Sakra (or Sakat) *brother of Rana Pratap of Mewar,* Kalla Kachhwaha and Lala son of Raja Birbar.[71]

Besides the lower grades in the Revenue Department, the Imperial service was primarily a military service and the major portion of the Hindu population had no interest in it. When we consider the percentage of Hindus in Akbar's service, we have to keep this in view.

Many Hindus rose to high posts in the Revenue Department. Raja Todar Mal[72] and Rai Pitr Das[73] rose to the highest post of the Chief Diwan or the Imperial Finance Minister. Rai Ram Das officiated as Diwan at the centre.[74] Of the four Deputy Finance Ministers appointed by Akbar at the centre under the Imperial Diwan, Qilich Khan, two were Hindus. Rai Pitr Das was concerned with the Province of Delhi. Rai Ram Das became Deputy Finance Minister for the Provinces of Agra, Allahabad, Bihar and Bengal.[75]

In 1595 Akbar divided the empire into five circles and each was put under a supervisor to see that no toll was collected anywhere. The region from Lahore to Gujarat was entrusted to Ram Das Kachhwaha.[76] When a similar inspection was instituted in 1601, the roads from the capital to Malwa and the Deccan were entrusted to Ram Das and the road to Gujarat to Kalyan Das.[77]

Krishn Das was appointed as Provincial Finance Minister of Bengal. Ram Das was Provincial Finance Minister of Bihar. Bharati Chand became Fianance Minister of the Province of Ajmer. Rai Ram Das was sent to Ahmadabad as Provincial Finance Minister of Gujarat. Khanur was Finance Minister of Avadh. Mathura Das was Provincial Finance Minister of the Province of Lahore. The Finance Department of the Province of Delhi was in the hands of Ram Rai. The Finance Ministry of the Capital Province of Agra was entrusted to Keshav Das.[78]

Akbar created work for Hindus in the Judicial Department as well. He instituted new courts with Hindu judges and a certain civil jurisdiction was assigned to them to decide cases according to Hindu law when both the parties were Hindus.[79]

Many Hindus were given important posts in the administrative services. When Akbar divided the work of the central government into several departments and every one of them was entrusted to a body of high officials, Hindus were also there to run the Imperial government. There were Rai Sal, Rai Surjan, Raja Todar Mal, Rai Durga, Jagan Nath, Lunkarn, Raja Askarn, Jagmal and Raja Birbar distributed among various departments.[80] Rai Purushottam[81] and Tara Chand[82] rose to be the Provincial Bakhshis of Bihar and Avadh respectively.

Raja Jagan Nath and Rai Durga were appointed as Joint Governors of the Province of Ajmer. Raja Askarn was a Joint Provincial Governor at Agra.[83] Raja Man Singh, Raja Bhagwan Das, Rai Rai Singh Bikaneri and Raja Todar Mal were appointed at various times as Provincial Governors.[84]

There were four Hindu governors during Akbar's reign of half a century and only one Indian governor during a century and a half of British rule. No Hindu in British India ever rose to the position of Todar Mal as the Central Finance Minister of India.[85] And the percentage of Hindu officers in Akbar's army was higher than the percentage of Indian officers holding the King's Commission in the British army in India before World War II.[86]

But Hindus had also identified themselves with Akbar. The line of demarcation was not between Hindus and Muslims. It was between the Emperor's friends and foes. They would fight against Hindus and Muslims alike. When Akbar attacked Chitor, Bhagwan Das accompanied him to fight against the Sishodhiyas. And Todar Mal with Akbar's famous engineer, Qasim Khan, was in charge of the siege constructions.[87] In 1574 Rai Singh of Bikaner was fighting against Rai Chandra Sen of Jodhpur.[88] When Akbar sent from Ajmer a strong expedition against Rana Pratap in 1576, Kunwar Man Singh was put in supreme command. He was accompanied by Jagan Nath, Khankar, Lunkarn and others. The Rana was defeated in the battle of Haldighati.[89] Rai Rai Singh attacked and subdued the Raja of Sirohi and Abugadh.[90] When Duda Chauhan of Bundi revolted against the Imperial authority, his own father, Rai

Surjan, and brother, Bhoj, with Ram Chand and Kurmsi and others marched against him, defeated him and captured the fort of Bundi.[91] Against Raja Madhukar Bundela of Orchha were sent Raja Askarn, Raja Udai Singh, and others.[92] In 1593 Raja Udai Singh of Jodhpur marched against the Raja of Sirohi.[93] Datman Das fled from the court and revolted. His own father, Ram Das, requested the Emperor to send an army against him.[94]

Muslims and Hindus in Akbar's service lived together, worked together, were put in charge together, were with their Emperor together, even in his privacy. He would not make any distinction. *Todar Mal*[95] and Muzaffar Khan worked together as Diwans.[96] Then the former worked with Diwan Khwaja Shah Mansur Shirazi.[97] Later he was to work as Diwan with Mir Fath-Allah.[98] *Rai Pitr Das Diwan* and Khwaja Shams-ud-Din Diwan were to co-operate with each other.[99] *Madhat Singh* was appointed as the Assistant Imperial Diwan to help Qilich Khan.[100] *Raja Askarn* and Shaikh Ibrahim were Joint Governors of the Province of Agra.[101]

When Raja Bhagwan Das fell ill in 1586 at Attak, Akbar sent to treat him Hakim Hasan and *Mahadev.*[102] When the news of the illness of his son-in-law, Mirza Shahrukh, reached him in 1602, *Beni Das* was deputed for his treatment.[103]

Not only in the Emperor's service, but also in that of his nobles there were Muslims and Hindus. A Zain-ud-Din Ali was in the service of a Man Singh,[104] a Ram Chand[105] in that of an Abd-ur-Rahman.[106]

Even when Akbar wanted to be away from the court ceremonials, his few companions used to be Muslims and Hindus. On his journey to Kashmir in 1589, when leaving his retinue behind he went ahead riding on horse and walking on foot, he would sit down under a tree and rest awhile with his companions, Khan-khnan, Zain Khan Kuka, Hakim Abu-l-Fath, *Jagan Nath,* Abul-Fazl, Mir Sharif Amuli, Qazi Hasan, Nur Qilich and *Ram Das.*[107]

If Hindus served and revered him, Akbar loved and honoured them. He would pay visits even to those who were not of high rank to honour them or to sympathise with them in their sorrows. When he was at Mathura, he went to the house of Mathura Das.[108] When the building of Birbar's palace was completed, he was honoured by a royal visit.[109] Todar Mal had desired the same for a long time. At last Akbar went to his residence and Todar celebrated the occasion.[110] To Birbar Akbar paid a second visit.[111] When Ram Das' son was killed, Akbar went to his house for condolence.[112]

Hindus were as dear to him as Muslims. Once two court wrestlers, a Hindu and a Muslim, *Jagsobha* and Haibat Tahamtan, were fighting in the arena. Contrary to the rules of sportsmanship, Haibat tore open the hand of Jagsobha. Akbar was infuriated and gave him a stunning blow.[113] One day Akbar and his courtiers were watching the fighting of elephants on the polo-ground. Suddenly one of the beasts ran after Birbar and was going to coil him in its trunk. Instantly, heedless of his own life, Akbar spurred his horse and galloped between the two.[114]

The Inner working of the System

The Rajputs would fight for the Imperial interests against Hindus and Muslims. But, in the absence of clannish strife, to fight against Rajputs in Rajputana was rather disconcerting, especially to take harsh measures against them. After the defeat of Rana Pratap at Haldighati, Man Singh entered his country and Mughul armies were stationed there. In the hilly country communications were difficult. The food became scarce and armies were on the verge of starvation. But Man Singh would not allow the Mughuls to plunder Rajput people, to rob them of their cereal subsistence. To allow that in Rajputana was too much for his Rajput honour. The situation became untenable and Muslim generals sent a report to the Emperor. Akbar, of course, could not afford to starve his armies. Man Singh was called back at once.[115] When Man Singh and Bhagwan Das were again sent to pursue the Rana, they were accompanied by Qutub-ud-Din Khan.[116] Next time Mirza Khan was to go with them.[117] A great practical man as he was, Akbar was able to grasp the situation. When Bhagwan Das and Man Singh with others were again sent to invade the Rana's country, the supreme command was given to Shahbaz Khan. Shahbaz, before he launched his attack, took extra precaution to avoid any half-heartedness. He sent back Raja Bhagwan Das and Man Singh to the court.[118]

Shahbaz was a general of pluck and daring, and a man of determination. Under his orders the mountainous tracts, deep ravines and hilly precincts all were trodden under the Mughul horses. He took the Kalvara pass and stormed the fort of Kumbhalmer. It fell and he pushed along. At midday surrendered Gogunda, at midnight Udaipur.[119] Shahbaz was equal to the task. Again and again he was given the same command. He would have completed the conquest of Mewar, but Akbar needed him elsewhere. Only when the hold of this great general from the Panjab was removed, Rana could come out of his mountain den and prowl around. Many years afterwards, when Akbar's hands were free, the same old Shahbaz was sent against the Rana.[120] A Shahbaz could not be half-hearted. Such was the policy which Akbar adopted regarding war in Rajputana.[121]

When a group of persons work together, a superior is needed to supervise them. When hundreds of people of various nationalities and different religions are put together, there are apt to be common sympathies and rival jealousies and a strong man is doubly needed to see that no one suffers. Akbar proved to be a vigilant supervisor. Todar Mal was very efficient in his work, but, at the same time, was of a very spiteful nature.[122] Once, when Shahbaz Khan came to the court, very hot words were exchanged over money matters between him and Todar Mal, who was the Central Diwan at that time. Akbar formed a board of four, consisting of Khan-khanan, Mir Fath-Allah Shirazi, Hakim Abu-l-Fath Gilani and Abu-l-Fazl, to investigate the matter. Neither proved just in his demands.[123] On another occasion we find Akbar taking out of prison Qazi Ali Baghdadi, who had been unjustly put there by the good offices of Raja Todar Mal.[124]

When Man Singh was Governor of Kabul, reports were received that his Rajput soldiers were behaving high-handedly towards the people and that he was not doing full justice to the matter. At once Akbar sent his transfer orders and Zain Khan Kukaltash was appointed Governor of Kabul.[125]

Akbar began to build his empire from Agra when most of Indian provinces like Bihar, Bengal, Malwa, Gujarat and others were in the hands of Muslim rulers. Akbar's Hindu generals felt no qualms in putting an end to their rule. Neither they had any hesitation in exterminating Muslim nobles who would rebel against the Emperor. They had no sympathy for them. Their own power against Akbar was insignificant. The result of any revolt on their part was a foregone conclusion. Akbar was, therefore, their only refuge. Their gains lay in his loyal service only. And we find them caring above all for the interests of the Emperor.

When Khanzaman openly rebelled in the East, Akbar himself marched against him and Mir Muizz-ul-Mulk, Lashkar Khan and Todar Mal were sent against his brother, Bahadur Khan. Khanzaman sued for peace. The Prime Minister, Munim Khan, interceded in his behalf and won Akbar's pardon for him.[126] But, in spite of the fact that Bahadur repeatedly requested for respite till the result of his brother's supplications was known, Todar Mal 'worked as oil on fire' and Mir Muizz-ul-Mulk attacked him.[127] Similarly, when Davud, King of Bengal, was defeated and he begged for peace, Munim Khan accepted his submission and allowed him to retain a few districts in Orissa. But Todar Mal would not agree to it. He was for his complete destruction.[128]

When Qaqshals, because of the undue severity and maltreatment of Muzaffar Khan, rebelled in Bengal, at one time the rebel leaders and Muzaffar's representatives met together to discuss peace terms. Among the latter was Rai Pitr Das. His men, Narayan Das Ghalot and others got ready to kill their adversaries in cold blood. But a Rizvi Khan, in spite of the fact that he was Muzaffar's representative, would not suffer it to happen. A hint from him was eloquent enough and 'the birds had flown away'.[129]

Akbar was aware of this intentional and incidental undivided loyalty of Hindus and availed himself thereof implicitly. He would trust them more than most others, especially when there was rebellious commotion under the surface. The Province of the Panjab occupied the most strategic position. It was first on the line of approach from the North West. Its resistance or submission to the invader was enough to decide the fate of the government at Delhi or Agra. At the time of Khanzaman's rebellion in the East, Mirza Hakim had already once ventured to cross the border. In 1578 Akbar assigned jagirs in the Panjab to the Kachhwahas, *Raja*[130] *Bhagwan Das, Jagan Nath and others.*[131]

Just a few months before the impending rebellion of 1579-81 he sent *Raja Bhagwan Das, Jagan Nath, Raja Gopal, Jagmal Patvar* and a few others to the Panjab to serve under Said Khan,[132] and they were directly ordered to do their utmost in organising (the administration and forces of) the province and keeping themselves ready (to move with their armies) at a moment's notice.[133]

The restiveness had been simmering. Mulla Tayyib and the new Bakhshi, Rai Purushottam, proved tactless in their exactions in Bihar, and Masum Khan Kabuli, Arab Bahadur and many other nobles broke out in open rebellion.[134] Muzaffar's demands in Bengal led Turkmans to rise in revolt under Baba Khan Qaqshal.[135] Akbar sent *Todar Mal* against the rebels in the East.[136] Soon after Khan-i-Azam and Shahbaz Khan were also sent there.[137]

Akbar expected Mirza Hakim's invasion from the North West. His forecast proved correct. Hakim's armies crossed the Indus. Akbar ordered *Man Singh* to go ahead and take charge of the frontier displacing Mirza Yusuf Khan. Man Singh hurried there and marched against Hakim's vanguard general, Shadman, who was defeated and fatally wounded by Man Singh's brother, *Raja Suraj Singh.* From Agra Akbar despatched reinforcements under *Rai Singh* of Bikaner.

Mirza Hakim crossed the Indus and entered Hindustan. Akbar left his capital and marched towards the Panjab.

Hakim reached Lahore and encamped outside the city. Within the city fort there were Said Khan, *Raja Bhagwan Das Kunwar Man Singh* and others who proved too strong for him.

When Hakim heard of Akbar's movements, he retraced his steps. But Akbar's march continued to Kabul.

After crossing the Indus Akbar left behind his main army in charge of Said Khan and *Bhagwan Das* with Prince Salim.

Kunwar Man Singh under Prince Murad of eleven[138] was sent in advance. He encountered the Mirza and defeated him.

After a short stay at Kabul Akbar marched back towards his capital.[139] Todar Mal returned to the court from the Eastern front with the tidings that the backbone of the Bihar rebellion had been broken.[140]

It was, no doubt, the most critical time in Akbar's career.[141] But the situation had been saved. Thanks to Akbar's powers of organisation and his cool calculating tactfulness in managing the wavering nobles. Thanks to his faithful Muslim nobles. Thanks to *all* of his Hindu nobles.

Such a critical situation never arose again. Still Akbar always utilized the services of his Hindu nobles most judiciously. They were appointed where the most trusted were needed. When he returned from Kabul, the charge of the North West frontier was entrusted to *Kunwar Man Singh.*[142] The Panjab was left in the hands of *Raja Bhagwan Das, Rai Rai Singh, Jagan Nath* and others under Said Khan.[143] Next year *Bhgwan Das* was appointed Governor of the Panjab.[144]

When Mirza Hakim died in 1585, *Man Singh* was ordered to hasten towards Kabul to take charge of the country and manage its affairs. Man did it well and returned to the court, leaving there his son, Jagat Singh.[145] *Bhagwan Das* was appointed Governor of Kabul. But when neither he nor his successor would willingly proceed to this difficult charge, *Man Singh* was again sent there as Governor.[146]

Bhagwan Das remained Governor of the Panjab for the rest of his life. All the time when Akbar was at Lahore after 1586 Bhagwan Das was in charge of the Emperor's Household.[147]

A second centre of rebellion was formed in the provinces of Bihar and Bengal. The rebel leaders there had been defeated and the revolt suppressed, but the East still required particular care. *Man Singh* was sent to Bihar in 1587 where he proved himself a successful Governor.[148] In 1594 he was appointed Governor of Bengal[149]—a position which he held for many years.

Sometimes Akbar entrusted to his Hindu nobles services of another kind. In 1599 Muhammad Yar, son of the daughter of Gulbadan Begum, the renowned sister of Humayun, left the court with rebellious intentions. To arrest him Akbar sent Salhadi and Dhanman Das.[150]

When Akbar was in the Deccan, Muzaffar Husain Mirza, son of Gulrukh Begum, daughter of Mirza Kamran, Humayun's brother, and his own son-in-law, husband of his daughter, Khanam Sultan, left the Imperial army with treasonable plans and rode away towards Gujarat. None of the nobles tried to arrest him. Akbar was much offended and sent Rai Durga and Rai Manohar to pursue the culprit.[151]

Hindu officials not only served Akbar, in a way they also rendered a great service to millions of Hindus in India. Their presence among the Imperial nobility and among the officials of the government was a great security for their co-religionists. Hindu Rajas would always seek protection of the Hindu 'umara',[152] who used to intercede in their behalf, recommend their cases or guarantee their safety at the court and help them or their representatives in every way they could. The messenger of the Raja of Kajli, near Malabar, presented himself in the court through Raja Birbar.[153] Bhupat Chauhan, a rebel of Etawa, a fugitive from the imperial soldiers, entered the Royal camp to seek forgiveness, because he was sure of the protection of Raja Todar Mal and Raja Birbar.[154]

When Khan-khanan, in Gujarat decided to attack the Jam, a local Hindu ruler, for his dishonest dealings and the latter entreated for peace, Rai Durga and Kalyan Rai of the Imperial army interceded in his behalf.[155] When Raja Madhukar of Orchha proved refractory and Shihab-ud-Din Khan marched out to punish him, it was through Raja Askarn and Raja Jagan Nath, who were in the Khan's army, that he came to pay his homage to the Khan and renew his allegiance.[156]

Raja Rudr of Kamaon was prepared to come and pay his homage to the Emperor, if Raja Todar Mal would take him under his protection. The Raja sent his son, Kalyan Das, to escort him to the court.[157]

Sometimes they would take the initiative and persuade the Rajas to come to terms and escape destruction. When Raja Basu of the Panjab hills behaved in a refractory way, an imperial force under Hasan Beg and others was sent against him. But

Raja Todar Mal wrote him a letter emphasizing the untoward consequences. Before the punitive force reached his place, he came out to see the general in charge and accompanied him to the court 'to illuminate his forehead by rubbing it on the ethereal threshold'.[158]

In a Feudal System the King's vassals were too powerful for him to allow their alliances. Hence the Royal prerogative to control their marriages. The Great Mughuls, though they never allowed their nobles to become French Dukes, were also very keen to control their matrimonial unions. The daughters of important 'umara' were married in the Royal family. These 'umara' were thus inseparably attached to the Emperor. Sometimes a favourite young noble was married to the daughter of some powerful grandee to strengthen his position in the court. The young Mirza Khan, future Khan-khanan, son of Bairam Khan, was married to Mah Banu Begum, sister of Khan-i-Azam Mirza Aziz Kukaltash.[159] A daughter of Mirza Aziz Kukaltash was married to Prince Murad;[160] a younger one was later married to Prince Khusrau.[161] Khan-khanan's daughter, Khan-khanan Begum, was married to Prince Danyal.[162] A daughter of Qilich Khan was also married to the same prince.[163] Hasan Qilich was married to the daughter of Asaf Khan.[164] Akbar allowed Prince Salim to marry 'a beautiful daughter' of Zain Khan Kuka.[165]

This control of marriages was not limited to Muslim 'umara' only. It was extended to Hindu nobles as well. Likewise their daughters were married into the Royal family and in the same way their marriages with one another were controlled. We find Akbar marrying the daughter of Ram Das to Syam Singh.[166] This would not have been an isolated instance.

Ladies of the umara's harems observed 'parda'. The only exception made sometimes was in the case of the emperor himself. On ceremonial occasions in the palace they would join in the celebrations and pay their homage to the emperor. Akbar introduced the Mina Bazaar[167] : on the Nauroz or the New Year Day Festival and monthly festal days ladies of the emperor's and the umara's harems would meet together in the Royal palace and a market was held where they used to sell and buy.

This was a social assemblage which, in addition to riding, hunting, falconry, sight-seeing and garden-visits, added to the liveliness of the female life. The Emperor himself would come to shop in these bazaars and chat with the shopkeepers and the customers. But his real motive used to be to know about them.[168] It was here that most of the matrimonial proposals originated which were later carried forward by the Emperor.[169] And these bazaars were attended by the ladies of the Rajput nobles' households as well.[170]

But Akbar's influence on his Hindu nobility was even greater than this. Not only did they accept his regulating their social life, they tolerated him even when their deep-rooted religious susceptibilities were touched. They accepted his interference, because they knew their Emperor. He did not interfere to contaminate their sacred customs. His wishes originated from love and humanity. He prohibited the 'sati'[171] of a widow if she was not willing to destroy herself,[172] and he would have his orders obeyed.

When Jai Mal, husband of the daughter of Raja Udai Singh of Jodhpur, died, his widow refused to undergo 'sati'. But such was the force of centuries old tradition that her own son determined to burn his mother alive and made preparations. When the news reached Akbar, he did not issue any order. He sprang upon his swiftest steed and galloped away. He rode hard. He reached there in time. The culprits were brought before him. He sent them to prison.[173]

At another time we find him dissuading a widow from undergoing 'sati'. Akbar would have, no doubt, liked 'sati' to disappear altogether. When the husband of Rai Rai Singh's daughter died, she determined on 'sati'. Akbar went to Rai Singh's to offer condolence and was able to persuade the lady not to destroy herself for the sake of her young children.[174]

The Cultural Contacts

If Akbar did not like Hindu 'sati', he liked many other things of Hindus. He enjoyed their epics and romances; he liked to know their religion and philosophy. *Nal-o-Daman, Singhasan Battisi, Ramayan, Mahabharat, Atharv Ved* and other

Sanskrit and Hindi books were rendered in Persian prose and poetry.

The story of the lover, Nal, and his beloved, Daman, was composed in Persian poetry by the Poet Laureate, Faizi.[175] *Singhasan Battisi*—Thirty-two Tales about Raja Bikrmajit of Ujjain—was written in Persian by Abd-ul-Qadir Badauni, the celebrated writer of the Religious History of Akbar.[176] *Ramayan*'s Persian version was also his work,[177] as well as *Adharv Ved*'s[178] *Mahabharat* was done in Persian by Naqib Khan, Badauni, Mulla Sheri and Haji Sultan Thanesari.[179] *Harivams, Lilavati* and *Panchtantra* were also translated into Persian.[180]

And among the saints and scholars of the age the Court Historian includes Hindu 'rishis' and 'vidwans' side by side with Muslim 'auliya' and 'ulama'.[181] Among the Hindu saints there were Madhav Sarswati, Madhusudan, Narayanashram, Harji Sur, Damodhar Bhat, Ramtirath, Nar Singh, Param Indra, Adit, Baba Bilas, Ram Bhadr, Jadurup and Narayan. The Hindu scholars included Madhav Bhat, Sri Bhat, Bishan Das, Ram Krishna, Ballabhdhar Misra, Basudev Misra, Bhan Bhat, Vidyanivas, Gauri Nath, Gopi Nath, Krishna Pandit Bhattacharya, Bhagirat Bhattacharya, Kashinath Bhattacharya, Vijai Sen Sur and Bhan Chand.[182]

Akbar had also begun to love Hindi names, which he would give to his war-elephants, horses, hunting cheetahs and weapons. Among his elephants there were *Bal Sundar,*[183] *Nainsukh, Jalpa, Gaj-gajan,* Khudabakhsh, *Panjpaya, Gaj Bhanvar,* Gardbaz *Dhokar, Madhukar, Jangiya, Sabdilya,* Qadra, Asmanshukoh, Fatoha, *Lakhna, Ranbagh, Kheri Singh, Gajpati, Bhairav, Khande Rai, Man Singh, Chitranand, Pandrik, Poska,* Mubarakqadam, *Chachar, Pavan, Ranmohan, Jagatrai, Gajmangal, Lakhmi Sunder, Mukut, Gaj Mukuta, Gaj Raj,* Ran Madar, Shahrukh, Fathlashkar, Lal Khan and *Haul Rai.*[184]

The names of three of his horses are mentioned as Nur-i-baiza, *Harprasahd* and Shahinayat.[185] His hunting cheetahs included Daulat Khan, Samand *Naik, Chitranjan,* Dilrang and *Madan* Quli.[186] The musket with which Akbar shot dead Jai Mal and Chitor fell was named *Sangram.*[187]

Akbar's court physicians and surgeons were Muslims and

Hindus alike. They included *Mahadev, Bhim Nath, Narayan, Shivji,*[188] *Biyarchu, Bhairav* and *Chandra Sen.*[189]

Akbar loved Indian music and most of his court musicians, including the most prominent ones, were Hindus or Indian Muslims carrying on the traditions of Hindu 'raags'.[190] There were *Mian Tan Sen.*[191] *Nanak Charju, Ram Das, Shihab Khan, Purbin Khan, Subhan Khan, Davud, Sur Das, Surgiyan Khan, Sarod Khan, Chand Khan, Mian Junaid Gawaliyar, Mian Lal, Rang Sen of Agra, Bichitar Khan, Tan Tarang Khan, Shaikh Dadan, Muhammad Khan, Mulla Ishaq Multani, Rahmat-Allah, Surmandal Khan,* Ustad Dost Mashhadi, Mir Sayyid Ali Mashhadi, Ustad Yusuf Haravi, Bahram Quli Haravi, Hafiz Khwaja Ali Mashhadi, Qasim Kohbur, Sultan Hashim Mashhadi, Tash Beg Qibchaq, Pirzada Khurasani, Ustad Shah Muhammad, Mir Abd-Allah, Sultan Hafiz Husain, Ustad Muhammad Amin and Ustad Muhammad Husain.[192]

It was in the court of Akbar that the Muslim and Hindu painters worked together and there evolved the famous Indo-Mughul painting. To estimate the contribution of the Indian discerning eye one may compare the uniform bulbous faces in most of the Persian Miniatures of the period with the individual features of various faces in many Mughul paintings. They had achieved perfect portraiture. The most distinguished of Akbar's painters were Mir Sayyid Ali Tabrizi, Khwaja Abd-us-Samad Shirazi, *Daswant,*[193] *Bisavan, Kesu, Lal, Mukund,* Miskin, Farrukh Qalmaq, *Madhav, Jagan, Mahesh, Khem Karn, Tara, Sanwla, Harbans and Ram.*[194] There were many others including *Bhagwati, Nana, Bandi, Tulsi, Bishan Das, Madhav Kochak,* Aqa Riza, Khusrau Quli, Jamshaid, *Kesu Khurd, Jagjiwan, Paras,* Ibrahim, *Bhim, Sur, Dhan Rai, Triya, Bhagwan, Chatish, Gobind, Banwari,* Mukhlis, Sharif, *Tulsi Kochak,* Chitr, two Muslim painters from Lahore, a few Hindus from Gujarat and some from Kashmir.[195]

One can see how far Akbar, his government and his court had been indianised. But this influence was not one-sided. Persian had been made the official language of the empire.[196] All the Hindus in government service from a Haft Hazari to a Mutasaddi had to learn it. The linguistic barriers thus broken, in the friendly atmosphere that Akbar created Hindus began to love Muslims and many things of Muslims. One of the Rajput generals of Akbar was Raja Lunkarn. His son's name was Manohar. But he was called Muhammad Manohar. He learned Persian so well that the began to compose verse in Persian. Akbar gave him the title of Mirza and he would be styled as Mirza Manohar. But his father loved his previous name so much and was so proud of it that he would still call him Muhammad Manohar.[197] Due to the repitition of *m*s and *h*s and both the parts of the combination being of equal syllables, it really sounds sweet when spoken aloud. But to relish its sweetness the Raja had first to cease to dislike and then, perhaps, to like the person whose name its first part originally was.

And how was this mutual cultural infiltration working? Lunkarn was a relative of Bhar Mal, Bhar Mal's daughter, the Empress, was, therefore, a relative of boy Manohar, and her son, Prince Salim, became Manohar's best playmate.[198] The Rajput relatives of Akbar would hear in the Royal palace the word *Muhammad* appended before the names of many children. If they too liked it, because they liked the children who bore it, and added it before the names of their own sons, it should not surprise us.

Raja Kalyan Mal of Bikaner had named one of his sons as Sultan Singh.[199] The name of another Hindu general in the Bengal army was Subhan Singh,[200] the first part being the word with which a Muslim begins his prayers five times a day.

Akbar was bringing Muslims and Hindus close together. There was no religious persecution. Everybody was allowed to follow the religion be liked. The Hindu festivals of Rakhi, Dasahra and Divali were also celebrated by the Emperor and his court. For the Emperor's birthday charities was adopted the Hindu ceremony of Tuladan.[201] There were no sumptuary laws after he himself began to rule. The Hindus were persianised and turkised. This unity of Muslims and Hindus, living together like brothers and influencing each other, giving rise to an Indo-Muslim culture and civilisation and a common language was the achievement of this Monarch.

The Reason Why?

Akbar is said to have 'tried to cement the differences between Hindus and Muslims by inter-communal weddings, making no distinction of caste or creed in the conferment of high titles and offices and above all by attempting to establish a new faith which should be the harbinger of a new world.'[202] It is also claimed that his policy towards Hindus was intricately connected with his later religious views.[203] But a survey of the chronological record of Akbar's religious beliefs and practices side by side with his measures which built his new polity for Muslims and Hindus and gave rise to a new cultural pattern does not confirm this popular view.

In 1561 Akbar, who was on his pilgrimage to the tomb of Khwaja Muin-ud-Din Chishti, at Ajmer, married the daughter of Raja Bhar Mal of Amber and enrolled Man Singh into the Imperial service.[204]

The Emperor, who promoted Todar Mal in the Revenue Department, appointed Shaikh Abd-un-Nabi Muhaddis, grand-son of the well known saint, Shaikh Abd-ul-Quddus Gangohi, as the Sadr, the Chief Justice of the realm who was also in charge of all the state endowments throughout the empire.[205]

On his birthday in 1565 Akbar was weighed against gold, silver, scents, cereals and other things according to *the Hindu* Royal ceremony of Tuladan and these were distributed among *the Brahmans* and others. But, at the same time, when some of the nobles at the end of the expedition against Khanzaman desired Akbar to forgive the culprit, those who were selected to intercede in his behalf were all '*ulama*'[206], Mir Murtaza Sharifi, Mulla Abd-Allah Sultanpuri and Shaikh Abd-un-Nabi Sadr, because he respected *their* wishes.[207]

The Emperor, who visited the tombs of saints at Delhi before the invasion of Ranthambhor and paid a visit to the tomb of the Ajmer saint after its capture, had entrusted *Todar Mal* with the whole work of 'wazarat' (the Finance Ministry) during its siege.[208]

Akbar, who begged saints for the life of his children and would send his expectant wives to the 'blessed' house of a saint for delivery, married the niece of Rai Kalyan Mal of Bikaner and the daughter of Raval Har Rai of Jaisalmer.[209]

In 1571 Akbar pressed his scheme of converting the obscure village of Sikri into a magnificent Imperial capital, because it was the home of a Muslim saint, Shaikh Salim Chishti.[210] But the style of the Royal palaces and other buildings constructed was an amalgamation of the Muslim and Hindu architectural traditions.

The Emperor gave the name of *Madan* Quli to one of the cheetahs he captured in 1571. He had named two of the elephants he captured in the jungles of Malwa as *Kheri Singh* and *Gajpati* in 1563.[211]

Akbar's war cry for many years was 'Allah-o-Akbar! Ya Hadi Ya Muin!', 'Allah-o-Akbar! Ya Hadi Ya Muin!'. The first was God's name to invoke His help and the second that of the Ajmer saint to call for his blessings. But to this repeated invocation Akbar had given the Hindi name of *suwiran*.[212]

The Emperor, who would vow to offer the Royal drums of his enemy at the tomb of a saint, if his arms were successful, appointed *Rai Bhagwan* as the Mustaufi-i-Mumalik (the Auditor General) at the centre and honoured *Todar Mal* with a banner and a kettle-drum.[213]

Akbar, who would keep awake most nights repeating 'Ya Hu! Ya Hadi! Ya Hu! Ya Hadi!', 'Help me my God! Help me my Guide!', who had such a respect for the Religious Dignitary, Shaikh Abd-un-Nabi, that he would go to the extent of placing the Shaikh's foot-wear before his feet with his own hands, who had declared that all who wished to go on Haj, the Mecca pilgrimage, could go at the state expense, appointed a Hindu as Mushrif-i-Diwan of the Empire and ordered the *Atharv Ved* to be translated into Persian.[214]

The Emperor, who was in the habit of saying his prayers five times a day and who would bid fare-well to his Mir-i-Haaj, the leader of the caravan of pilgrims to Mecca, putting on 'ihram' and having his hair cut as the pilgrims do when they approach the 'Kaba', with one sheet round his loins and another round his body with his right shoulder uncovered, and walking along with him for some distance, bare-footed and bare-headed, with a heart full of love and reverence and tears trickling from his eyes, married the daughter of the Raja of Dungarpur.[215]

Every important step that the Emperor took during the 1570s was taken after consultation with the Ecclesiastical Head of the Empire, the Sadr, Shaikh Abd-un-Nabi. Todar Mal was appointed as Diwan or the Imperial Finance Minister in 1577.[216]

By the year 1578 the famous Hindu painters of Akbar's court, Bisawan, Kesu and Sanwla had definitely entered his service and were working for him.[217]

We can see that the process of Akbar's policy towards Hindus had not begun through his political sagacity by the year 1578, thereafter to be completed by his changed religious views in later years, as Sharma says.[218] It had practically been completed in all its beneficial features by that time.

All that for which Akbar stands in history—toleration of all religions, equal citizenship for all subjects, recognition of merit, eligibility of one and all for every post, even the highest, in the state service and appreciation of everything appreciable, Muslim or Hindu—was not due to any deviation from Islam on his part. It was the work of a keen-sighted statesman.

NOTES

1. V.A. Smith, *Akbar, The Great Mogul,* p. 58.
2. Ibid, 63.
3. Ibid, 58.
4. Abu-l-Fazl, *Akbarnama,* Bibliotheca Indica, Vol. ii, p. 20.
5. Ibid, 45.
6. *Akbarnama,* ii, 45 بر زبان غیب ترجمان گذشت که «ترا نهال خواهیم کرد» و همچنان شد
7. Sons of Raja Bhar Mal's brothers, Askarn and Jagmal respectively. (*Akbarnama,* ii, 155-56)
8. *Akbarnama,* ii, 155-56.
9. *Akbarnama,* ii, 156.
10. Ibid, 157.
11. Ibid, 157-58.
12. *Akbarnama,* iii, 606.
13. Ishwari Prasad, *Medieval India,* p. 264.
14. *Akbarnama,* iii, 743.
15. *Akbarnama,* ii, 156.
16. The Husband-selection ceremony in which princes showed their feats of valour and the princess garlanded the prince whom she

chose for her husband.

17. Tod, *Annals of Boondee,* cited in *Akbar, The Great Mogul,* V.A. Smith, p. 99.
18. *Akbarnama,* ii, 155.
19. Ibid, 197.
20. Ibid, 161-62.
21. *Akbarnama,* ii, 190.
22. کهان
23. *Akbarnama,* ii, 358.
24. Ibid, 358-59.
25. *Akbarnama,* iii, 196, 210.
26. P. Saran, *The Provincial Government of the Mughals,* pp. 143-44.
27. *Akbarnama,* iii, 451.
28. Ibid, 494.
29. Ibid, 603.
30. P. Saran, *The Provincial Government of the Mughals,* p. 146.
31. *Akbarnama,* iii, 699.
32. *Akbarnama,* iii, 572.
33. Ibid, 581.
34. Ibid, 826.
35. Ibid, 54, 61, 56, 49.
36. هرگاه ملازمانِ ما درین نبرد مرد آزمائی خود را ببرهنگی قرار دهند از مردی نباشد که ما مسلح باشیم. *Akbarnama,*iii, 49
37. Bhang : an intoxicant made of Indian hemp.
38. *Akbarnama,* iii, 49-50.
39. Their loyalty became well-known even abroad. When Mirza Hakim marched against Akbar in 1581, in the rumours of defection set afloat only Irani and Turani armies were said to change sides on the battlefield. (*Akbarnama,* iii, 366)
40. Abd-ul-Qadir Badauni, *Muntakhab-ut-Tawarikh,* Bibliotheca Indica, Vol. ii, p. 210.
41. Ibid, 276.
42. *Akbarnama,* iii, 372.
43. Ibid, 606.
44. Ibid, 763.
45. Ibid, 747-48.
46. In italics : Names of Hindu officers and rulers.
47. *Akbarnama,* ii, 265.
48. Ibid, 291.
49. Ibid, 373.
50. *Akbarnama,* iii, 43.
51. *Akbarnama,* iii, 19.

52. Ibid, 43.
53. When he was only eighteen years old.
54. Sri Ram Sharma, *The Religious Policy of the Mughul Emperors,* p. 18.
55. How much they were interested in the fate of their weak sons-in-law is well illustrated by Raja Ajit Singh of Jodhpur. In spite of the fact that his daughter was married to Farrukh-siyar, he was one of those who compassed his destruction.
    (William Irvine, *Later Mughals,* Vol. i, p. 408)
56. *Akbarnama,* ii, 164-65,
57. Ibid, 170.
58. Ibid, 193.
59. Ibid, 228.
60. *Akbarnama,* ii, 261-62.
61. Hemu's rise to power was due to foreign invasion and Adil's incapacity.
62. *Muntakhab,* ii, 66.
63. جواب داده‌اند که «هرکدام شما در سرکارِ خود هندوئی دارید. ما هم هندوئی داشته باشیم - چرا ازو بد باید بود؟»
    Muntakhab-ut-Tawarikh, ii, 66
64. See Appendix B.
65. *Muntakhab,* ii, 228.
66. *Akbarnama,* iii, 815.
67. Nizam-ud-Din Ahmad, *Tabaquat-i-Akbari,* Bibliotheca Indica, Vol. ii, p. 480.
    Panj Hazari—Holding the Mansab of the Commandant of Five thousand cavalry.
    Haft Hazari—Holding the Mansab of the Commandant of Seven thousand cavalry.
    Chahar Hazari—Holding the Mansab of the Commandant of Four thousand cavalry.
    Do Hazari—Holding the Mansab of the Commandant of Two thousand cavalry.
    Yak Hazar Panj Sadi—Holding the Mansab of the Commandant of One thousand and Five hundred cavalry.
    Yak Hazari—Holding the Mansab of the Commandant of One thousand cavalry.
    Haft Sadi—Holding the Mansab of the Commandant of Seven hundred cavalry.
    Sih Hazari—Holding the Mansab of the Commandant of Three thousand cavalry.
    Do Hazar Panj Sadi—Holding the Mansab of the Commandant of Two thousand and Five hundred cavalry.
68. Abu-l-Fazl; *Ain-i-Akbari,* Bibliotheca Indica, Vol. i, pp. 222-31.

Tabaqat, ii, 425-56.
Akbarnama, iii, 839, 786, 837, 820, 836, 809, 834, 832, 826.

69. Panj Sadi—Holding the Mansab of the Commandant of Five hundred cavalry.
Chahar Sadi—Holding the Mansab of the Commandant of Four hundred cavalry.
Sih Sadi—Holding the Mansab of the Commandant of Three hundred cavalry.
Do Sadi—Holding the Mansab of the Commandant of Two hundred cavarly.
70. Most probably. He is mentioned as Jai Mal of Mirtha (*Akbarnama*, iii, 81) and the Defender of Chitor is said to have been in command at Mirtha before he came to Chitor. (V.A. Smith, *Akbar, The Great Mogul*, p. 88)
71. *Ain*, i, 222-31.
72. *Akbarnama*, iii, 381.
73. Ibid, 741.
74. Ibid, 80.
75. Ibid, 605.
76. Ibid, 670.
77. Ibid, 801.
78. *Akbarnama*, iii, 670.
79. *Muntakhab*, ii, 356.
80. *Akbarnama*, iii, 404-5.
81. *Muntakhab*, ii, 281.
82. *Akbarnama*, iii, 511.
83. Ibid, 511.
84. *Akbarnama*, iii, 492, 525, 651, 397, 491, 717, 198.
85. He also worked as the 'Vakil' or the Vicegerent of the Emperor. (*Akbarnama*, iii, 381.)
86. Sri Ram Sharma, *The Religious Policy of the Mughal Emperors*, p. 27.
87. *Akbarnama*, ii, 316, 320.
88. Ibid, 81.
89. Ibid, 166.
90. Ibid, 196-97.
91. *Akbarnama*, ii, 201.
92. *Akbarnama*, iii, 210.
93. Ibid, 641.
94. Ibid, 788.
95. In Italics: Names of Hindu officials.
96. *Akbarnama*, ii, 197, 333, 336.
97. *Akbarnama*, iii, 215.

98. Ibid, 457.
99. Ibid, 741.
100. Ibid, 570.
101. Ibid, 511.
102. Ibid, 492.
103. *Akbarnama,* iii, 815.
104. Ibid, 336.
105. Zain-ud-Din Ali and Ram Chand were generals in command, not menials.
106. *Akbarnama,* iii, 792.
107. Ibid, 538.
108. Ibid, 373.
109. Ibid, 397.
110. Ibid, 440.
111. Ibid, 438.
112. Ibid, 789.
113. *Akbarnama,* iii, 328-29.
114. Ibid, 436.
115. *Tabaqat,* ii, 326. *Akbarnama,* iii, 185, 190.
116. *Akbarnama,* iii, 191.
117. Ibid, 196.
118. Ibid, 218.
119. Ibid, 238-39.
120. Ibid, 749.
121. It was only in Rajputana that the hand of the Rajputs hesitated. Elsewhere they proved more imperialist than the Emperor himself. When Man Singh was Governor of Bihar, he marched against Raja Puran Mal and defeated him (1590). The best of his elephants and choicest presents he secured from him as well as his daughter for his brother, Chandra Bhan. Then he proceeded against Raja Sangram. He submitted. After sometime he attacked Raja Anant Charva and collected abundant spoils.

    When in Orissa, Man Singh went on pilgrimage to Jagannath (1592). But it was also to cover his approach to Raja Ram Chand for attacking him at an opportune moment. The 'thought was translated into action' and the Raja was forced to submit.

    When Man Singh was appointed Governor of Bengal and Orissa, he required the tributary Raja, Ram Chand, of Khurda, in Orissa, to come and pay him homage (1593). But the latter refused to pay homage to a Governor. Man Singh at once despatched an army against him under his son, Jagat Singh. Jagat besieged the fort of Khurdagadh and devastated the outlying country. Many places like Sejpal, Kharagadh, Kalubara, Khanan, Lungadh and Bhawanmal were taken. When Akbar heard of this wanton aggression, he reprimanded Man Singh and asked him to recall his forces and apologise to the Raja. (*Akbarnama*, iii, 576, 615, 631).

122. *Akbarnama,* iii, 158, 569,
123. Ibid, 529.
124. Ibid, 571.
125. *Akbarnama,* iii, 517-18.
126. *Muntakhab,* ii, 79, 82. *Akbarnama,* ii, 260
127. Ibid, 80, 81, Ibid, 261.
128. *Akbarnama,* iii, 130-31.
129. Ibid, 293-94.
130. In Italics: Names of Hindu generals.
131. *Akbarnama,* iii, 248.
132. Ibid, 262.
133. و فرمان شد که در لوازمِ خدمت گذاری جد گزین آمده ... در انتظامِ آن صوبه و آمادگی و خود زمانی نغنوند *Akbarnama*, iii, 262
134. *Muntakhab,* ii, 281 *Akbarnama,* iii, 284.
135. Ibid, 280. Ibid, 290-93.
136. *Akbarnama,* iii, 287.
137. Ibid, 308, 314.
138. *Muntakhab*, iii. 294 که حکم شاه بچهٔ شطرنج کبیر داشت
139. *Akbarnama,* iii, 335-70.
140. Ibid, 372.
141. *Akbarnama*, iii, 343 و وقتِ نازک
142. *Akbarnama,* iii, 372.
143. Ibid, 372.
144. *Akbarnama,* iii, 397.
145. Ibid, 467-73
146. Ibid, 491-92.
147. Ibid, 525.
148. Ibid, 525.
149. Ibid, 651.
150. Ibid, 651.
151. Ibid, 771.
152. Umara: nobles.
153. *Akbarnama*, ii, 341-42.
154. *Akbarnama,* iii, 279.
155. Ibid, 454.
156. Ibid, 526.
157. *Akbarnama,* iii, 533.

158. Ibid, 510.
159. Ibid, 747.
160. Ibid, 518.
161. Ibid, 806.
162. Ibid, 837.
163. Ibid, 647.
164. Ibid, 799.
165. Jahangir, *Tuzk-i-Jahangiri*, p. 8. صبيهٔ صاحبِ جمالِ زين خان كوكه
166. *Akbarnama*, iii, 799.
167. *Ain*, i, 200.

    Abu-l-Fazl does not give the name, Mina Bazaar, to these lively markets. They formed part of the annual New Year Day Festival, the Jashn-i-Nauroz, and the monthly merrymaking, the Khushroz (*Ain*, i, 200) The name was not yet coined perhaps.
168. *Ain*, i. 200.
169. *Muntakhab*, ii, 339.
170. In the Treaty of Bundi, 1569, (Tod, *Annals of Boondee*, cited in *Akbar, The Great Mogul*, V.A. Smith, p. 99) one of the terms is that the ladies of the House of the Prince of Bundi would be exempted from taking part in the Mina Bazaar on the Nauroz Festival. The Nauroz Festival or Mina Bazaar did not exist at the time. Hence the later invention of the Treaty. But it evidently implies that the ladies of the Hindu umara's households used to take part in it after its introduction (in 1582. –*Akbarnama*, iii, 379).
171. Sati : burning the widow alive on the funeral bier of her dead husband.
172. *Muntakhab*, ii, 376.
173. *Akbarnama*, iii, 402.
174. Ibid, 641.
175. Ibid, 661.
176, *Muntakhab*, ii, 183.
177. Ibid, 366.
178. Ibid, 212.
179. Ibid, 320. *Muntakhab*, iii, 252, 118.
180. Sri Ram Sharma, *The Religious Policy of the Mughal Emperors*, 25, 62.
181. Rishis : Saints.

    Vidwans: scholars.

    Auliya : saints.

    Ulama : scholars.
182. *Ain*, i, 233-35.
183. In italics : Hindi names.

184. *Akbarnama*, ii, 291, 293, 295, 75, 286, 294, 321, 60, 150, 233, 235, 234, 334, 294.
 Akbarnama, iii, 239, 92, 436, 820, 365, 174, 175, 819, 815, 107.
185. *Akbarnama*, iii, 101, 823, 824.
186. Ibid, 94, 45. *Akbarnama*, ii, 371, 363.
187. *Akbarnama*, ii, 320.
188. *Ain*, i, 234.
189. *Tabaqat*, ii, 484.
190. Raags : Melodies. Six primary Melodies are Bhairav, Maalav, Saarang, Hindol, Vasant and Deepak or Megh.
191. In italics : Names of Indian musicians—Hindu or Muslim.
192. *Ain*, i, 236-64.
193. In italics : Names of Hindu painters.
194. *Ain*, i. 117.
195. Laurence Binyon, *The Court Painters of the Grand Moguls*, pp. 46, 69, 70.
 Percy Brown, *Indian Painting under the Mughals*, pp. 65, 114, 115, 116, 118, 121, 122, 123.
196. *Khallaq-us-Siyyaq*, cited in *The Religious Policy of the Mughal Emperors*, Sri Ram Sharma, 62.
197. *Muntakhab*, iii, 201-2.
198. *Tabaqat*, ii, 452.
199. *Akbarnama*, iii, 158.
200. Ibid, 611.
201. *Ain*, i, 197.
 Tuladan : The Emperor was weighed against gold, silver, scents, some metals, minerals, silk, cereals, etc. and these goods were entrusted to a man in-charge and an accountant to be given away in charity to the needy, Hindus and Muslims, during the ensuing year (*Ain*, i, 97).
202. S.R. Sharma, *The Mughal Empire in India*, vol. i, p. 327.
203. Sri Ram Sharma, *The Religious Policy of the Mughal Emperors*, 23.
204. *Akbarnama*, ii, 156-58.
205. *Muntakhab*, ii, 66, 71.
206. Ulama : Scholars well-versed in Islamic learning.
207. *Muntakhab*, ii, 83-84. *Akbarnama*, ii, 268.
208. *Akbarnama*, ii, 334, 336. *Tabaqat*, ii, 224.
 Akbarnama, ii,336 حل و عقدِ وزارت باو مفوض بود
209. *Akbarnama*, ii, 343-44, 358-59.
210. Ibid, 365.
211. Ibid, 363, 233, 235.

212. *Akbarnama*, iii, 51, 55.
213. *Tabaqat*, ii, 299.
     Akbarnama, iii, 87, 103.
214. *Muntakhab*, ii, 200, 204, 212.
     Tabaqat, ii, 312-13.
     Akbarnama, iii, 158.
215. *Muntakhab*, ii, 247, 238-39.
     Tabaqat, ii, 327.
     Akbarnama, iii, 196.
216. *Akbarnama*, iii, 233, 213.
217. Percy Brown, *Indian Painting under the Mughals*, 114.
218. Sri Ram Sharma, *The Religious Policy of the Mughal Emperors*, 23.

Appendix A

Akbar is said to have tried to cement the differences between Hindus and Muslims by inter-communal weddings, making no distinction of caste or creed in the conferment of high titles and offices and above all by attempting to establish a new faith which should be the harbinger of a new world. It is also claimed that his policy towards Hindus was intricately connected with his later religious views. But a survey of the chronological record of Akbar's religious beliefs and practices along with his measures which built his new polity for Muslims and Hindus and gave rise to a new cultural pattern does not confirm this popular view. It shows Akbar's current religious beliefs and practices when he introduced these measures and proves that their introduction was not the result of any deviation from Islam on his part.

Akbar : 1561-1578

1561 Akbar on pilgrimage to the tomb of Khwaja Muin-ud-Din Chishti at Ajmer.

" The Emperor accepted Raja Bhar Mal's Matrimonial alliance.

1562 The Emperor married the Amber princess.

" Man Singh enrolled in the Imperial service.

" Bhagwan Das and his relatives in the Emperor's service.[1]

" Raja Buddhi Chand in Government service.[2]

1562 Todar Mal in the Emperor's service.[3]

" Raja Kapur Dev and Raja Ram Chand in the Imperial service.[4]

" Tan Sen, the famous Indian musician, called to the court from Gwalior.[5]

1563 Todar Mal and Rai Pitr Das serving the Emperor on the battle-field.[6]

" Akbar captured elephants in the jungles of Malwa. Two of the elephants engaged in the hunt were *Khande Rai* and *Bhairav*. Two of the elephants captured were named by Akbar as *Kheri Singh* and *Gajpati*.[7]

Todar Mal promoted in the Revenue Department.[8]

" Abd-un-Nabi, grandson of Shaikh Abd-ul-Quddus, a well known saint of India, appointed as Sadr, the Chief Justice of the realm, who was also in charge of all state endowments throughout the empire.[9]

" Akbar visited the tomb of Khwaja Nizam-ud-Din at Delhi.[10]

" The Emperor arranged for the Mecca pilgrimage of Humayun's wife, Haji Begum.[11]

1565 Todar Mal a general.

" Serving on the battle-field : Raja Mitr Sen, Kurmsi, Rai Pitr Das and Rai Sal.[12]

" One of those put in charge of the Imperial army : Raja Bhagwan Das.[13]

" On his Birthday the Emperor weighed against gold, silver, scents and cereals according to the Hindu Royal ceremony of Tuladan and these goods distributed among the *Brahmans* and others.[14]

1565 Akbar respected the wishes of the 'ulama': Mir Murtaza Sharifi, Mulla Abd-Allah Sultanpuri and Shaikh Abd-un-Nabi Sadr.[15]

1566 The Emperor paid a visit to the tombs of saints at Delhi.[16]

" Again he visited the tombs of saints at Delhi to beg their support against Khanzaman.[17]

" Hindus in the Emperor's service : Bhagwan Das, a general; Nathwa Mehra, a scout; Som Nath, an elephant-keeper; Bansi Das, an executioner.[18]

1567 Todar Mal : a grandee of the Empire.[19]

-68 Serving the Emperor during the siege of Chitor : Bhagwan Das, Todar Mal and Rai Pitr Das.[20]

" The Emperor after the fall of Chitor proceeded towards Ajmer, travelling last stages of the journey on foot, to proffer his thanks to the Khwaja for this victory.[21]

" Akbar went to Narnaul to see Shaikh Nizam and sought his blessings.[22]

" The Emperor entered Chitor riding on his elephant, Asmanshukoh. Among the elephants with him there were Gardbaz *Dhokar*, *Madhukar*, Jangiya and *Sabdilya*.[23]

1568 Before marching against Ranthambhor the Emperor visited the tombs of saints at Delhi to entreat their support.[24]

" Akbar paid a visit to the tomb of his favourite saint at Ajmer.[25]

1568 The Emperor visited the Chishti saint, Shaikh Salim, at Sikri and sought his blessings for the life of his children. A few children born before all had died in infancy.

1568-69 Akbar sent his expectant Queen, daughter of Raja Bhar Mal, to the blessed house of Shaikh Salim Chishti for delivery.

" The Emperor built a new monastery for the Shaikh and a beautiful mosque nearby at Sikri.[26]

" During the siege of Ranthambhor Todar Mal put in charge of the whole work of 'Wazarat', the Finance Ministry.[27]

Akbar attended the Muslim religious ceremony of the funeral dinner of Darbar Khan.[28]

1569-70 August 30, 1569, The Rajput Queen gave birth to her son in the house of a Muslim saint. This grandson of Raja Bhar Mal was named Salim after Shaikh Salim Chishti.

" The happy father, in pursuance of his vow, started on foot towards Ajmer to offer his thanks to the Khwaja.[29]

" From Ajmer Akbar proceeded towards Delhi to visit the tombs of saints at that place.[30] Besides others there were the tombs of Khwaja Qutb-ud-Din, successor of the Khwaja of Ajmer, and Khwaja Nizam-ud-Din, who had inherited his ministry from Khwaja Farid-ud-Din of Pakpattan, the Successor of Khwaja Qutb-ud-Din.

" Kavi Rai Brahm Das (future Birbar) prominent in the court.[31]

1570 Another prince, Murad, born in the blessed house of Shaikh Salim Chishti.

" Akbar marched towards Ajmer, because he must visit the tomb of Khwaja Muin-ud-Din Chishti at least once a year.[32]

" From Ajmer Akbar proceeded towards Pakpattan to visit the tomb of Khwaja Farid-ud-Din.[33]

" The Emperor on his way to Pakpattan was waited upon by Rai Kalyan Mal of Bikaner and accepted the latter's proposal to marry his niece. He also accepted the proposal of marrying the daughter of Raval Har Rai of Jaisalmer.[34]

" Kalyan Mal's son, Rai Singh, enrolled in the Imperial service.[35]

" From Pakpattan Akbar marched towards Dipalpur. The Emperor captured six cheetahs on the way. The finest of them he named as *Madan* Quli.[36]

1571 The obscure village of Sikri was converted into a great capital by the Emperor, because he wished to add imperial grandeur to the spiritual splendour of the home of Shaikh Salim Chishti.[37] But the style developed for the Royal palaces and other buildings was an amalgamation of the Muslim and Hindu architectural traditions.

1572 Akbar went to Ajmer and entreated the Khwaja to grace his invasion of Gujarat.

" The Emperor paid a visit to Mir Sayyid Husain Khingswar's tomb near Ajmer.[38]

" Akbar on campaign against Gujarat. The capital left in charge of *Raja Bhar Mal.*[39]

1572 On his march against Gujarat the Emperor received at Nagaur the tidings of the birth of another prince in the blessed house of Shaikh Danyal, a 'mujavir' (attendant) at the tomb of the Ajmer saint. He named him Danyal after the Shaikh and he was wished to become "the Defender of the Faith of the Prophet".[49]

" The Emperor ordered the newly-born prince to be brought up under the care of the *Rani of Raja Bhar Mal.*[41]

" Serving in the Gujarat campaign : Bhagwan Das, Man Singh, Bhupat Kachhwaha, Rai Singh Bikaneri and others.[42]

" Kavi Rai given the title of Raja Birbar.[43]

" During the Gujarat campaign the Emperor hunted at times as usual. A cheetah was set upon a deer. There appeared in front a wide ravine. Up jumped the deer to cross it. Up jumped the cheetah and brought it down. The Emperor was much pleased at this unparalleled feat. He installed it as the King of Cheetahs and drums were ordered to be beaten before its carriage whenever on the move. This princely cheetah was *Chitranjan.*[44]

1573 From Gujarat Akbar proceeded towards Ajmer. He paid his devotions to the Khwaja and requested his blessings in his every undertaking.[45]

" Todar Mal sent to study the Mughul military position in the East and submit a report thereon.[46]

1573 The emperor marched against Gujarat once again. The capital entrusted again to *Raja Bhar Mal.*[47]

" On his way Akbar visited Ajmer to beg the favours of the Khwaja.[48]

" When the Gujarat battle raged, Akbar would cry.
"Allah-o-Akbar! Ya Hadi Ya Muin!,
Allah-o-Akbar! Ya Hadi Ya Muin!"[49]

" Hindus who served the Emperor in the Gujarat expedition : Raja Bhagwan Das, Rai Rai Singh, Jagan Nath, Rai Sal, Jai Mal, Jagmal Patvar, Raja Dip Chand, Man Singh Darbari, Ram Das Kachhwaha, Ram Chand, Sanwal Das, Jadun Kaisth, Duwar Bhalla, Har Das, Tara Chand, Karn, Rupsi, Salbahan, Ranjit, Hapa Charan and Raghu Das Kachhwaha.[50]

" The Experor returned from Gujarat. Todar Mal sent to Gujarat to assess its land revenue.[51]

" On his way back Akbar again visited Ajmer to offer his thanks to Khwaja Muin-ud-Din Chishti for his victories in Gujarat.[52]

" Parmanand put in charge of the Imperial war-boats and artillery.[53]

" On one Friday Akbar was present in the Cathedral Mosque at Fathpur to say his Friday prayers. The preacher in the pulpit referred to the idolatory of the Prophet's parents and their consequent punishment. Akbar declared, "Undoubtedly this statement hasn't any truth in it. When myriads of people are going to be absolved of their sins at the intercession of the Prophet, it is unbelievable that his own father and mother should be deprived of the mercy of Allah."[54]

1573 The Emperor ordered the debts of Saif Khan Kuka and Shaikh Muhammad Bukhari, who had been killed in the Gujarat battles, to be cleared from the Royal treasury "to remove this burden from their life hereafter."[55]

" In the second Gujarat expedition when Akbar asked Saif Khan Kuka and Mirzada Ali Khan not to attack a lion and endanger their lives, he swore by "the Sacred Dust"[56]—the Dust of Madina.

" Todar Mal sent to the East to expedite operations against Bengal. Generals on the front were required to treat him as the Emperor's Supervising Representative.[57]

" Rai Ram Das appointed to officiate for Todar Mal as Diwan at the centre.[58]

" At the end of the month of Ramazan Akbar celebrated the Islamic festival of 'Id'. In the assemblage Khwaja Abd-ush-Shahid, grandson of Khwaja Nasir-ud-Din Abd-Allah Ahrar, was sitting in a corner. The Emperor seated him beside himself.[59]

1574 Akbar proceeded to Ajmer to entreat the Khwaja for the success of his arms against Davud of Bengal. He was accompanied by his five years old son, Prince Salim. The little prince also offered his prayers at the tomb of the Khwaja.[60]

" The Emperor marched towards Patna. From his way he sent a large sum of money to the village of Munir for distribution among the people at the tomb of Shaikh Yahya Muniri.[61]

1574 From Patna Akbar proceeded towards Delhi to visit the tombs of saints there.[62]

" Davud defeated. From Delhi Akbar went to Ajmer. He offered his fulsome thanks to the Khwaja and presented two of the Royal drums of Davud at the tomb, which he had vowed to do before the beginning of the war. While in Ajmer the Emperor was mostly in the company of the 'ulama' and 'mashaikh' or in the assemblies of 'sama' at the tomb.[63]

" Rai Bhagwan appointed as the Mustaufi-i-Mumalik (the Auditor General) at the centre, displacing Tayyib Khan.[64]

" Rai Purushottam : a Bakhshi.[65]

" Munim Khan despatched to conquer Bangal. Todar Mal sent with him after having been honoured with a banner and a kettle-drum.[66]

" Badauni ordered to translate into Persian "Singhasan Battisi"—Thirty-two Tales about Raja Bikrmajit of Ujjain.[67]

1575 Bhavan, a Brahman, embraced Islam. He became one of the closest friends of the Emperor.[68]

" The construction of the Ibadatkhana or the House of Discussions ordered.[69]

" For Ibadatkhana the 'hujra' (cubicle) of Shaikh Abd-Allah Niyazi Sarhindi, a former disciple of Shaikh Salim Chishti, was rebuilt and extensions were added to it.[70]

1575 The Emperor loved the company of the 'ulama' and 'mashaikh' and religious discussions[71], which he considered a part of worship.

" Akbar kept awake most nights repeating "Ya Hu! Ya Hadi! Ya Hu! Ya Hadi!", his heart filled with awe and love of the Almighty.[72]

" Akbar would go out before daybreak and sit on a plank of stone in solitude, in all humility, in deep meditation ('muraqaba') with his eyes closed and his head bent upon his chest.[73]

„ The building of the Ibadatkhana completed. On Thursdays in the evening and on every Friday after the congregational prayers Akbar held religious discussions therein, which continued till daybreak.[74]

„ The Emperor had deep respect for Shaikh Abd-un-Nabi. He would go to his house to listen to his discourse on the 'Hadis'. Once or twice he placed with his own hands the Sadr's shoes on the ground before him when the Sadr wanted to wear them.[75]

„ Akbar sent Prince Salim to the 'hujra' of the Shaikh to learn the 'Chihl Hadis'.[76]

„ A Royal farman issued: the 'aimma' (priests in mosques) throughout the empire were not to be given the proceeds of the 'madad-i-maash' lands or any stipend unless they produced a new farman to this effect from the Sadr, Shaikh Abd-un-Nabi.[77]

„ After the conquest of Gujarat and the capture of its seaports the Emperor decided to send every year a caravan of pilgrims to Hijaz from Hindustan at the state expense under his own Mir-i-Haaj.

1575 Akbar's aunt, Gulbadan Begum, and his wife, Salima Sultan Begum, prepared to go on pilgrimage to the 'Haramain' (Mecca and Madina). The Emperor declared that all who wished to join them could have the expenses from the Royal treasury.[78]

„ Shaikh Abd-un-Nabi and Makhdum-ul-Mulk ordered to assess Jizya upon Hindus.[79]

„ Qazi Jalal and other 'ulama' asked to write a commentary on the Quran.[80]

„ Badauni ordered to translate the *Atharv Ved* into Persian.[81]

„ Todar Mal appointed the 'Mushraf-i-Diwan' at the centre.[82]

1576 Akbar proceeded to Ajmer. The last fifteen miles of the journey travelled on foot in honour of the Khwaja as usual. Akbar took Kunwar Man Singh with him within the sepulchre of the Khwaja, had a talk with him in private, and begged the Khwaja for his support in the ensuing war in Mewar. Then he gave the robes of honour to Man Singh and sent him in command of fifteen thousand soldiers, Hindu and Muslim, against Rana Pratap. Other Hindu generals who accompanied Man were Jagan Nath, Madhav Singh, Khankar and Rai Lunkarn.[83]

" The Rana defeated. Akbar proceeded to Ajmer for thanksgiving service at the Khwaja's tomb and reached there on the day of Khwaja's 'urs' (death anniversary).[84]

" The Emperor ordered his workshop to manufacture a fine 'doshala' specially for Shaikh Abd-un-Nabi.[85]

1576 Akbar was possessed by an ardent desire for pilgrimage to Mecca and Madina. But the cares of kingship would not allow his absence. He asked his Mir-i-Haaj, Sultan Khwaja, to perform Haj on his behalf. The Khwaja was given twelve hundred robes and six hundred thousand rupees to distribute among the deserving at the 'Haramain'. The Emperor announced that all who wished to go on Haaj could go at the state expense.[86]

" Akbar, putting on 'ihram', bareheaded and barefooted, as if approaching the Kaba, bade farewell to Khwaja Sultan. His heart was full of love and reverence and tears were trickling from his eyes. Those who saw him thus were also moved.[87]

" Akbar at this time was in the habit of saying his prayers 'ba jamaat' five times a day.[88]

" The emperor married the daughter of the Raja of Dungarpur.[89]

1577 Akbar proceeded to Ajmer to visit the tomb of the Khwaja. On the way, at Mirtha, he bade farewell to his Mir-i-Haaj, Shah Abu Turab. Once again he declared that anybody could go on the Mecca pilgrimage free of charge.[90]

" At Ajmer Akbar attended the assemblies of the 'ulama', 'darvishes' and 'sama'.[91]

" On his return journey from Ajmer Akbar visited Narnaul to see Shaikh Nizam Narnauli. Here also he attended the 'sama'.[92]

1577 From Narnaul Akbar came to Delhi where he visited the tombs of saints. he also visited the tomb of his father, Humayun—a visit which he never omitted whenever at Delhi.[91]

" From Delhi Akbar proceeded to Hansi where he saw Shaikh Jamal Hansvi.[94]

" Akbar repeated at this time "Ya Hadi! Ya Hadi!" day and night.

" The Emperor named Badauni's son as Abd-ul-Hadi.[95]

" Mulla Abd-Allah Sultanpuri appointed as the Provincial Sadr of the Panjab.[96]

" Akbar sent Prince Murad himself to escort Maulana Muhammad Amin Yazdi to the house of Shaikh Abd-um-Nabi. The Shaikh was asked to help the Maulana, because the former had been given complete patronage of the 'mashaikh' and 'ulama'.

" Every important step was taken by the Emperor after consultation with Shaikh Abd-un-Nabi.[97]

" Todar Mal was appointed Diwan at the centre.[98]

1578 From Hansi Akbar proceeded towards Pakpattan to visit the tomb of Khwaja Farid-ud-Din.[99]

" From the Panjab Akbar started for Ajmer, where he reached in time for the Khwaja' 'urs'. The Emperor's return to Fathpur.[100]

" While at the capital, most of the time Akbar used to be in the company of the 'ulama' and 'mashaikh' in the Ibadatkhana where religious discussons were held. On Thursdays these discussions continued from evening till day-break.[101]

1578 Khwaja Muhammad Yahya appointed as Mir-i-Haaj and given four hundred thousand rupees for distribution among the 'mashaikh' and 'ulama' of the Holy Cities.[102]

" Todar Mal put in charge of the Bengal Mint. The Emperor carried out the reform of the mints in consultation with Todar Mal and Khwaja Abd-us-Samad Shirazi Shirinraqam, the chief artist and calligraphist of the court.[103]

By 1578 the famous Hindu painters of Akbar's court, Bisawan, Kesu and Sanwla, had definitely entered his service.[104]

And the 'ulama' did not object to Akbar's policy of co-operation and inter-communal weddings. They did not consider it harmful for the Muslim Faith or the Muslim State. When they did object, it was later and to something very different. Rather they co-operated with the Hindu officials. When Raja Bhar Mal was the Emperor's 'Vakil' at the capital, during the time of the first Gujarat campaign (1572), Makhdum-ul-Mulk Mulla Abd-Allah Sultanpuri worked with him as 'Wazir'.[105]

When Akbar marched towards Patna in 1574, he was accompanied by Raja Bhagwan Das, Kunwar Man Singh, Shaikh Abd-un-Nabi and Qazi Yaqub at the same time.[106]

The Muslims, even the 'ulama', would gladly accept the command of a Hindu general. They considered themselves as if fighting under Akbar himself.[107]

And once, when Kunwar Man Singh was given a military charge, Mulla Sheri wrote an 'Ode to the Emperor' in which he said,

"Such is the exaltation of our Faith,
Due to your justice, My Lord!
That even the Hindu has began
To wield the Sword of Islam."[108]

NOTES

1. *Akbarnama*, ii, 156-58. *Tabaqat*, ii, 155 *Muntakhab*, ii, 50.
2. Ibid, 164-65.
3. Ibid, 170.
4. Ibid, 193.
5. Ibid, 181.
6. Ibid, 228.
7. Ibid, 233-35.
8. *Muntakhab*, ii, 66.
9. Ibid, 71.
10. *Akbarnama*, ii, 201.
11. Ibid, 243.

12. Ibid, 216-62.
13. Ibid, 265.
14. *Muntakhab*, ii, 83-84.
15. *Akbarnama*, ii, 268.
16. Ibid, 276. *Tabaqat*, ii, 202.
17. Ibid, 288.
18. Ibid, 291-295.
19. Ibid, 299.
20. Ibid, 316, 320.
21. Ibid, 324. *Tabaqat*, ii, 220.
22. *Muntakhan*, ii, 104. Ibid, 221.
23. *Akbarnama*, ii, 321. *Muntakhab*, ii, 104.
24. Ibid, 334.
25. *Tabaqat*, ii, 321. *Muntakhab*, ii, 108.
26. *Akbarnama*, ii, 343-44. *Tabaqat*, ii, 225. *Muntakhab*, ii, 108-9.
27. Ibid, 336.
28. *Tabaqat*, ii, 225.
29. *Akbarnama*, ii, 349-50. *Tabaqat*, ii, 227. *Muntakhab*, ii, 123-24.
30. Ibid, 351. Ibid, 227. Ibid, 124.
31. Ibid, 341-42.
32. Ibid, 353, 356. *Tabaqat*, ii, 228-29. *Muntakhab*, ii, 132-33.
33. Ibid, 358. Ibid, 229-30 Ibid, 133.
34. Ibid, 358-59.
35. *Tabaqat*, ii, 230. *Muntakhab*, ii, 133
36. *Akbarnama*, ii, 363.
37. Ibid, 365.
38. Ibid, 371-72. *Tabaqat*, ii, 236. *Muntakhab*, ii, 139.
39. *Akbarnama*, iii, 19.
40. *Akbarnama*, ii, 373. *Tabaqat*, ii, 237. *Muntakhab*, ii, 139-40.
41. Ibid, 373.
42. *Akbarnama*, iii, 5-6, 11, 14. *Tabaqat*, ii, 238. *Muniakhab*, ii, 140.
43. *Tabaqat*, ii, 256. *Muntakhab*, ii, 161.
44. *Akbarnama*, ii, 371.
45. *Akbarnama*, iii, 38. *Tabaqat*, ii, 255-56.
46. Ibid, 41.
47. Ibid, 43.
48. Ibid, 44. *Muntakhab*, ii, 165.
49. Ibid, 51, 55.
50. Ibid, 49-56.
51. Ibid, 65.
52. Ibid, 65. *Tabaqat*, ii, 274.
53. Ibid, 70.

54. Ibid, 74.
55. Ibid, 73.
56. Ibid, 45.
57. Ibid, 71.
58. Ibid, 80.
59. Ibid, 78.
60. *Tabaqat*, ii, 277-79. *Muntakhab*. ii, 171-72. *Akbarnama*, iii, 79.
61. *Akbarnama*, iii, 94.
62. Ibid, 110. *Tabaqat*, ii, 298-99. *Muntakhab*, ii, 184.
63. Ibid, 110. Ibid, 299. Ibid, 185.
64. Ibid, 87.
65. Ibid, 87.
66. Ibid, 103.
67. *Muntakhab*, ii, 183.
68. Ibid, 212.
69. *Akbarnama*, iii, 112. *Tabaqat*, ii, 310. *Muntakhab*, ii, 198.
70. *Muntakhab*, ii, 201.
71. Ibid, 200.
72. Ibid, 200.
73. Ibid, 200.
74. *Tabaqat*, ii, 311-12. *Muntakhab*, ii, 201-2.
75. *Muntakhab*, ii, 204.
76. Ibid, 204.
77. Ibid, 204.
78. *Tabaqat*, ii, 312-13. *Muntakhab*, ii, 213.
79. *Muntakhab*, ii, 210.
80. Ibid, 211.
81. Ibid, 212.
82. *Akbarnama*, iii, 158.
83. Ibid, 163-65. *Tabaqat*, ii, 320-21. *Muntakhab*, ii, 227-28.
84. Ibid, 184-85. Ibid, 325. Ibid, 238.
85. *Muntakhab*, ii, 237.
86. *Akbarnama*, iii, 191-92. *Tabaqat*, ii, 325-26. *Muntakhab*, ii, 238-39.
87. *Tabaqat*, ii, 327. *Muntakhab*, ii, 238-39.
88. *Muntakhab*, ii, 247.
89. *Akbarnama*, ii, 196.
90. Ibid, 216-17. *Tabaqat*, ii, 334. *Muntakhab*, 251.
91. *Tabaqat*, ii, 334.
92. Ibid, 335. *Muntakhab*, ii, 252. *Akbarnama*, iii, 227.
93. Ibid, 335-36. Ibid, 252. Ibid, 228.
94. Ibid, 336. *Akbarnama*, iii, 232.
95. *Muntakhab*, ii, 252.

96. *Akbarnama*, iii, 234.
97. Ibid, 232-33.
98. Ibid, 213.
99. *Tabaqat*, ii, 337. *Muntakhab*, ii, 253. *Akbarnama*, iii, 236.
100. Ibid, 339. Ibid, 254. Ibid, 251.
101. Ibid, ii, 339. *Muntakhab*, ii, 255. *Akbarnama*, iii, 252-53.
102. Ibid, 341. Ibid, 267. Ibid, 264.
103. *Akbarnama*, iii, 227.
104. Percy Brown, *Indian Painting under the Mughals*, 114.
105. *Muntakhab*, ii, 151.
106. *Akbarnama*, iii, 87,
107. *Muntakhab*, ii, 228.
108. Ibid, 233. Azad, *Darbar-i-Akbari*, 770.

چنان رونق گرفت از عدل تو دین   که هندو می‌زند شمشیرِ اسلام

In the Melting-Pot

Chapter II

The Religious Headship

Humayun was an intensely religious man. Hamida, Akbar's mother, was the daughter of a learned and saintly father. The domestic atmosphere could not fail to affect the boy. He grew up to be a religious young man. His emotional nature and compassionate heart added zest to this sort of life. He was ever attached to the tombs of saints where there was food for his soul—intense worship and the best of devotional music.

Akbar had to fight against odds from the very beginning. He would entreat God for help and beg the favours of saints. When he won his struggles, the religious Emperor began to think his success the result of a 'Special Favour of God'. Successive victories and repeated escape from danger developed the idea that he was 'the Chosen of the Lord'.

Akbar was only twelve years old when he became an orphan, and an orphan on the throne. The regent soon became intolerably over-bearing. The situation was depressing. Akbar would seek solitude and sit alone in melancholy contemplation.[1] He was not allowed adequte funds. His elephants, his main entertainment, were snatched away from him.[2] Old nobles of his father were being put to death one after another. Tardi Bed had been sentenced to death; Khwaja Mahmud's death was compassed.[3] Akbar's helplessness was complete. The Queen Mother determined to fight for her son's rights. They had to fight against a stronger enemy. But they won the battle and the Grand Regent fell.

After the fall of Bairam Khan the influence of Maham became supreme. Her son, Adham, misbehaved and Akbar had to connive at even murders at their hands.[4] He became as helpless as before. He turned to his God for help.

He tried to see if God was not displeased with him.

Mounting a giant elephant he set it to fight against a vicious brute of its kind. Over the ground and over the river one pursued the other. The bridge of boats submerged and swayed. But the Royal rider was firm and safe on the neck of his elephant. The fight was over; the savages were tamed. He was convinced: God did not want his death; he was to live; he was to accomplish his task; his Lord would go with him.[5]

One night he was riding from Agra to Fathpur. Near the villages of Mandhakar some musicians were singing. Akbar listened; the spell of music worked on him. They were singing the praises of Khwaja Muin-ud-Din Chishti. Akbar decided to visit his tomb at Ajmer. He went there, proffered his supplications and begged the saint to secure the support of God for him.[6]

'The Chosen of the Lord'

At this time the dacoits of Sakit, about sixty miles from Agra, were strong in their eight villages and had become notorious for their forays. Akbar happened to go a-hunting in that direction. They had recently robbed a Brahman and killed his son. On the Emperor's approach the Brahman sought redress. With nearly two hundred men who were with him at the moment Akbar marched against them. Instead of begging his forgiveness, being four thousand in number, they strengthened their positions. Akbar ordered the assault and goaded his elephant to ram a wall himself. He fought so bravely that his Faujdar, Allaval Khan, who could not see his face behind the shield, cried out in applause, "Who are you, Brave man? Let me know your name. I shall commend you to my Emperor." Akbar removed his shield a bit from his face and Allaval recognised him. Seven arrows reached Akbar's shield and five of them pierced it through. But not one reached his body. He was doubly convinced: it was the Grace of God that shielded him.[7]

Khan-i-Azam Shams-ud-Din Muhammad Atga Khan after his return from the Panjab in 1561 became the Emperor's Chief Minister. Adham Khan, Maham's son, and a few others grew jealous of him. Adham had him killed in the Royal palace where he was working and then armed with sword he proceeded towards the Emperor's residence. The eunuch at the gate suspected him of treasonable intentions and locked the door. Akbar, who was sleeping inside, was aroused by the noise and came to know what had happened. Just when he was coming out of the door one of the harem maids gave him his sword. By chance he did not take the door outside which Adham was standing. When the Emperor approached him, Adham got hold of both of Akbar's hands and began to argue. The Emperor let his own sword go, released his hand and stretched it out to get Adham's sword. Instantly Adham's hand turned towards it. But before his hand could reach it, swordless Akbar had given him a blow in the face and knocked him down senseless. He was bound and twice thrown down from the top of the rampart. His neck was broken and his head was crushed. It was, Akbar believed, not his own hand but that of God that gave the blow.[8]

A second attempt on his life at Delhi next year also failed. An arrow that struck him on the right shoulder injured him slightly, but his assailant, Qatlaq Fulad, was cut to pieces on the spot. Akbar felt 'he was being protected by the Grace of God and the blessings of the favourites of God.'[9]

The traitors around him failed in their mission, but there were also traitors abroad. The chief of them was Ali Quli Khan Uzbek, the man who defeated Hemu in the battle of Panipat and was rewarded with the title of Khanzaman and the governorship of Jaunpur. A most intrepid soldier and a successful general, he was not an ordinary noble in rebellion. His following was large. His relations with many of the nobels of the court were intimate. His repeated submission had ever been opportune. He had been the refuge of malcontents from the Emperor's court. His right-hand man was his younger brother, Bahadur Khan, a playmate and class-fellow of Akbar himself. When Mirza Hakim invaded Lahore in 1566 and Akbar marched towards the Panjab, the Uzbek brothers rebelled once again and the 'khutba' was read in the name of Mirza Hakim. As soon as the news reached Lahore, Akbar had made his final decision: the young Emperor of less than twenty-five marched in person against the seasoned general to put an end to this trouble for ever.[10] Akbar was full of self-confidence. On the way, when two of his prominent elephants died suddenly and some people took it as ominous, he remarked, 'Nay, their death is of good augury. Both the wretches will be killed in the ensuing battle.'[11]

When Akbar heard about Khanzaman's presence in the vicinity and decided to attack him at once, he had to cross the Ganges. The river was in flood. But Akbar rode in his elephant. And 'the fierce water gave way!–due to the sheer good fortune of the Emperor.' It was 'a clear sign of his triumph.'[12]

Just before the battle the war-elephant, Khudabakhsh, calmed down and 'faujdars' and 'filbans' were sorry for it. But Akbar was optimistic. He said, 'If the elephant has come to its senses, it foretells our victory. Because the victory is always for the sensible', and then he added, 'Due to its calming down we have lost faith in elephants and their war-temper. Our sole dependence in this battle now is on the help of God, and whosoever trusts Him is ever successful.'[13]

Akbar was successful. The 'victory was for the sensible'. The 'clear sign of his triumph' proved true. Both 'the wretches were killed in the battle.' Akbar's trust in his God and confidence in his own self became tenfold.

In 1567 Akbar besieged the fort of Chitor. The siege protracted and there was tough fighting. Akbar himself directed the siege. Where the shots of muskets and cannon fell thickest he would walk slowly and complacently. One day a big shot from the enemy cannon fell near him. Twenty of his men were killed. But he was safe. 'His God was taking care of him.'[14]

Akbar marched out to conquer Gujarat in 1572. On the way he received the good news of the birth of another son at Ajmer and took it as an auspicious omen foretelling his victories in the west.[15] By this time he had become so confident of the strength of his arms that he had taken on this march to battle his harem and babies with him.[16]

After the surrender of Ahmadabad Akbar marched against the rebel, Ibrahim Hussain Mirza, in Baroda. The Mirza left the fort of Bharoch and was passing the Imperial camp at the distance of about twenty-four miles. The news was brought to

Akbar at midnight. Most of the generals had already been despatched to various directions. Akbar decided to attack the Mirza himself and started at once. The main army was left behind. Akbar would not allow more than forty men to go with him. He did not want to scare away the enemy. When he was earnestly entreated by his nobles to have more men with him, he replied, 'My trust in God assures me that I won't need armies to get rid of this rebel.'[17]

After some time Ibrahim Mirza was reported to be in the town of Sarnal, about twelve miles away on the other side of the river, with a large army. It was afternoon. Akbar consulted his men. A 'shabkhun'[18] was suggested. He did not like this dishonest dealing. He was for an attack before night. They had to gallop hard. To his companions he shouted, 'Take courage, my friends, take courage!' With forty men he was going to attack hundreds! They reached the river bank and there put on armour. On the other side stood Sarnal, on the top of a ridge. Here they were joined by men Akbar had sent for. All together they came to about two hundred. The Emperor rode his horse into the deep water. 'All praise to God! Due to the sacred self of the Emperor it proved fordable.'[19]

The scene of the battle outside Sarnal was a ground rifted into narrow lanes fenced with prickly cactus. No two horsemen could ride side by side. In the heart of the battle, when Akbar had only one companion, he was attacked by three soldiers. One of the assailants was engaged by his companion. But the other two turned on him. He spurred his horse, galloped over the cactus hedge and attacked them. They retreated and fled away 'in terror of the heavenly power that attended his arms.'[20]

The Mirza was defeated. Akbar was victorious. 'Human power could not achieve it. It was due to the Special Favour of God.'[21]

But when Akbar had returned to the capital, the Mirzas rallied their forces again and Aziz Kuka, the Governor left in charge of Gujarat, was unable to cope with the situation. He wrote to Akbar for help. The Emperor marched out at once. With swift camelry Akbar was traversing the desert of Central India.[22] Near the village of Jitaran a black deer was sighted.

Akbar said, 'If Samand Naik cheetah hunts down this deer, Muhammad Husain Mirza will fall into our hands.' The cheetah was set on and the deer was killed.[23]

Akbar wished to take the shorter route through Sirohi. The nobles insisted upon the safer route through Jhalaur. He would not listen to them, because 'his trust in God was firm and he ever expected His help in need.'[24]

In nine days this young Alexander of Hindustan covered six hundred miles of desert and on the eleventh his three thousand men were encamped against twenty thousand of the enemy. He shunned the suggestion of a 'shabkhun' and ordered his men to beat the drums of battle. He commanded his forces to cross the river which lay between them and their enemy. His nobles requested him to wait till reinforcements arrived from Pattan. He refused their advice. They entreated him to remain on this side of the river. He did not agree. They talked of the enemy's superiority in numbers. He replied, 'In every undertaking I place my faith in the Lord. In this expedition my sole help comes from Him. If I had thought of worldly means of success, I would not have come to fight with a handful of men in a distant land like this. Now when the enemy is ready for war in front of us, to stand and wait does not behove us.'[25] The nobles still hesitated to cross the river. But Akbar rode his horse into the water and they had to follow him. 'As soon as the Emperor entered the river, it became shallow.'[26]

Akbar called for his helmet. It was brought to him. The piece meant for covering the nose and a part of face had fallen off on the way. He said, 'All right. An auspicious sign. We shall also remove what is in front of us.'[27] When the enemy approached quite close, his men and he himself unsheathed their swords and attacked them crying, 'Allah-o-Akbar! Ya Muin! Allah-o-Akbar! Ya Muin!'[28]

Thrice he was personally attacked. Thrice he was able to repulse his assailants. The first of them struck the head of his horse and maddened it with pain. Akbar got hold of its neck and hurled his lance at the enemy. The second approached and tried to strike his thigh. The third came and threw his lance at him. But Akbar came safely through, unhurt, uninjured.[29] The battle was won. Muhammad Husain Mirza had fallen a prisoner in his hands.

Akbar was offering thanks to his God and only a few men were around him when suddenly there appeared a huge force with hundreds of war-elephants. Muhammad Husain's ally, Ikhtiyar-ul-Mulk, was approaching. All were allarmed except the Emperor. Bhagwan Das and a few others with him were not steady in shooting arrows. Akbar said, 'Don't lose your equilibrium. Await the help of God. Soon they will bring in his head.'[30]

And this actually happened, for Ikhtiyar-ul-Mulk's galloping horse struck a hedge of cactus and crashed to the ground with him. Suhrab Turkman reached the spot and cut off his head.[31] The help of God had come!

Akbar's trust in God and himself had become intoxicating. Successive events had confirmed it. He had begun to think himself invincible. At Patna, in 1573, he invited Davud, the Afghan king of Bengal, Bihar and Orissa, to a duel—'the country will belong to one who, by the will of God, comes out victorious.' Davud would not accept the offer.[32]

Patna fell and Akbar entered the city. Leaving the main army behind he decided to pursue Gujar Khan, the chief general of Davud. The river Panpan which had to be crossed was in spate. Many of the fleeing Afghans, in spite of the fact that they knew the river quite well, had just been drowned. But Akbar plunged his horse into the river. His men had to follow him. 'But they were crossing the river in the company of the Good Fortune of the Emperor.' Not a single man was lost.[33]

Such was Akbar of thirty—favourite of events, product of accidents, protege of victories: creature of circumstances, religious and devout, who considered himself 'the Favourite of God', 'the Chosen of the Lord'.

Akbar was interested in religious discussions. He had filled his court with 'ulama'. When Badauni, an 'alim',[34] was presented in the court, in 1573, he was introduced as a smart debater, 'a mace for the head of Haji Ibrahim Sarhindi', the chief of the court scholastic debaters. Akbar asked Badauni to assail certain views of Haji Ibrahim and the Haji was to defend them. The

Emperor himself played the judge.[35]

The same fondness for scholastic debates led the Emperor to order the construction of the 'Ibadatkhana' in 1574. The building was completed next year and debates began to take place there in right earnest. Akbar was zealous in worship and considered the discussion of religious topics a part of worship.[36] But he had begun to play with dangerous material.

Scholastic, legal and religious discussion, where the sole authority is quoting and interpreting writers of the past, may yield a very elastic form of argument. Most of the priestly class were too proud of their scholarship to accept one another's views. The respect and influence they enjoyed as religious pontiffs had corrupted many of them. The weight of their support when given being amply rewarded, many of them in the court service would not hesitate to distort 'the clear rulings of religion' to confirm Royal actions. Set against them were those courageous spirits who would make no concession to the Emperor's wishes. There were, moreover, the usual petty jealousies of human nature and the tactlessness of the martyrs. all this soon caused trouble and led to Akbar's estrangement from the priestly class.

Distrust in the 'Ulama'

First of the there arose dissatisfaction about the precedence in the seating arrangement and Akbar had to allot different sections to different classes.[37] The discussions themselves would degenerate into loud wrangles and reiterated irrelevance. Akbar was much annoyed and appointed a man to report misbehaviour.[38]

The large number of his wives seemed to weigh heavy on the Emperor's religious mind. He sought opinion on this point.[39] He was not prepared to divorce his wives other than any four[40] of them. He knew that a Shia could have more than four wives. He did not want to become a Shia either. But he wanted the legalization of his marriages all the same.

The 'ulama' might have put their heads together and tried to find out (as it was actually done afterwards) some solution of his problem. But they, especially the more important like

Abd-un-Nabi, Makhdum-ul-Mulk and Qazi Yaqub, would not help him out of his difficult position. They might not have liked the sham proceeding adopted later to overcome this difficulty. Consequently, the Emperor was much displeased with them.[41]

A way of escape was found out for him at last. Besides ordinary marriage, once there was made a provision for a marriage of another kind, primarily for soldiers who were kept fighting away from home for long. Under this provision soldiers were allowed to contract a marriage at the place where they were on active service on the understanding that it could be terminated when they returned home. The children were, of course, the liability of the father. There was laid no limit to the number of such marriages as it depended upon one's periods of long military service at different places, which, of course, could not be expected to be more than one or two in early life. Neither was there any compulsion to terminate such a marriage. Imam Aazam, seeing the system abused, declared it illegal. Availing oneself of this provision one could have, besides four wives, as many more wives as one liked to have and still remain within the letter of the law. Such marriages were called 'muta' marriages. They were permissible in the Maliki system of Sunni Fiqah and were quite common among the Shias.

Sunni Muslims recognise the authority of every one of the four Founders of Imams of the four Systems of Sunni Fiqah (Jurisprudence) for their respective followers. But, if in a country at a certain time the highest jurist authority, the chief Qazi, belonging to one of the systems pronounces a certain practice permitted in his own system legal for all, it becomes so for the followers of other systems as well, in spite of the fact that it is illegal according to their own system. This provision for uniform legal procedure in a state was pointed out to Akbar by Badauni, a Hanafi like Abd-un-Nabi and Mukhdum-ul-Mulk.[42]

Akbar was a Hanfi or follower of Imam Aazam Abu-Hanifa. So was the highest jurist authority in his realm, Quzi Yaqub. Akbar dismissed him and appointed in his place Qazi Husain Arb Maliki, a follower of Imam Malik. He pronounced the legality of 'muta' marriages for all throughout the empire. Akbar's marriages were thus legalized.[43]

But Qazi Husain Maliki, soon after he had performed the happy duty entrusted to him, was replaced by a Hanafi again, Qazi Jalal-ud-Din Multani.[44] Akbar perhaps did not like others to follow in his own footsteps. He was legalizing old marriages. Others might contract new ones.

At this time Akbar favoured the Quranic words, 'Allah-o-akbar', which mean 'God (Allah) is great (akbar)', to be engraved on the Royal Seal and become legend on his coins. He invited juristic opinion on this issue. Most of the 'ulama' consented to it. But Haji Ibrahim remarked, "It is better if the words, 'Remembrance of God is great',[45] are used. The phrase, God is akbar (great), might be taken as if conveying the sense: Akbar is God." Akbar replied that there was no question of his claiming to be God and added that he liked the phrase simply because the word 'akbar' was included in it and it was in praise of God.[46] A religious expert like Ibrahim must say something in matters religious. That was the trouble. Akbar did not like Haji's remarks.[47]

Meetings in the Ibadatkhana were after all social gatherings of human beings and soon human traits entered therein. Pungent humour began to spice the discussions and Akbar began to enjoy it. Thus encouraged those who were in Royal favour began to defame their opponents.Consequently the latter themselves and the class they represented were discredited in the eyes of Akbar.

Makhdum-ul-Mulk Abd-Allah Sultanpuri[48] was much respected and was called Shaikh-ul-Islam. He had been in the good books of Akbar himself. At the time of the invasion of Gujarat in 1572 he was left behind at the capital as 'Wazir' with the 'Vakil', Raja Bhar Mal of Amber.[49] Now he began to be slighted in the Ibadatkhana discussions. One night Khanjahan talked about Makhdum-ul-Mulk's ruling that the pilgrimage to Mecca was no longer binding on Indian Muslims, because, if one went by land, one had to hear unworthy things about the Companions and the Wives of the Prophet from the Shias in Persia, and if one went by sea, one had to get from the Portuguese a security-writ bearing the images of Mary and Christ and this was as if countenancing image-worship.[50]

Another interesting statement about him related how he had invented clever arrangement to escape the payment of 'zakat'. The 'zakat' is one fortieth of one's capital which has been in one's hands for the last twelve months. Makhdum-ul-Mulk, it was said, handed over all his wealth to his wife before the end of a year and took it back before the next year had run out. Many other similar stories defamed him.[51]

The other religious dignitary was Shaikh Abd-un-Nabi, the Sadr. Not only were his opponents active against him, but he himself also became a victim of wealth and power. Akbar had ordered in 1575 that no endowments or stipends were to be allowed unless the farman or the warrant had been inspected and renewed by the Sadr. Thousands of people from all parts of the country, therefore, flocked to the capital. Even the biggest Amirs would go to see the respected Sadr to request the renewal of the endowment of some good man they respected. The Emperor had given him the *carte blanche*. His powers demoralised him. He did not choose to decide the cases of the multitude awaiting outside his Sadr Court day after day, month in and month out. Away from their homes, strangers in Agra, their plight was miserable. Only those succeeded in their objects who could either bribe his subordinates or bring in the recommendations of some noble of the court. His attitude towards others was also becoming haughty and lacking respect.[52] Akbar was not unaware of these discreditable proceedings.[53]

Shaikh Mubarak and Abu-l-Fazl

But in the Ibadatkhana discussions there had already entered a disturbing element. In 1575 Abu-I-Fazl presented himself in the court for the second time and entered the Emperor's service. His elder brother, Faizi had already joined the court as a poet. Relations between their father, Shaikh Mubarak, and Akbar had become intimate after Faizi's entrance in the court. His influence was now doubly established. He was not in the court permanently, but would often visit the Emperor.

The religious discussions in the court so far had no guiding motive working behind them. They were ends in themselves.

The intellectual wranglers would fight to win a point. With the entry of Abu-l-Fazl in these discussions there entered a motive,[54] slowly, cautiously but very dexterously worked out. Shaikh Mubarak might assume the airs of a saint who had renounced the world and Abu-l-Fazl might talk monotonously about his intense desire to renounce the world, but they were quite mundane, worldly-wise. They would humour and amuse the emperor, study his every desire and talk and work accordingly. When Abu-l-Fazl came to the court for the second time, he presented to the Emperor a book, an interpretation of a section of the Quran. To please the Emperor it had been named *Tafsir-i-Akbari*–The Akbarian Commentary.[55] When the question of the number of wives a Muslim could legally have was in hot dispute, Shaikh Mubarak compiled a treatise citing all authorities in favour of the Emperor and his worthy son brought it to the court and placed it before the 'ulama' and the Emperor.[56] Their motive was, however, human and quite natural. They had suffered at the hands of Makhdum-ul-Mulk and Abd-un-Nabi.[57] They desired their downfall.

When Abu-l-Fazl came to the court, in 1575, and proved a striking debater in the Ibadatkhana discussions, Akbar was much pleased. The Emperor had become fond of this intellectual entertainment. He would back the young debater against the veteran 'ulama'.[58] By the year 1578 Abu-l-Fazl, with Shaikh Mubarak working behind the scene and with Akabar's moral support, had completely defeated and discredited Abd-un-Nabi, Makhdum-ul-Mulk and the other 'ulama' on their own ground of religion.

The conduct of the 'ulama' themselves also contributed to their downfall. When Akbar asked Qazi Jalal and other 'ulama' to write a commentary on the Quran, on every point they would differ and create noisy controversies.[59] The relations between Abd-un-Nabi and Makhdum-ul-Mulk became extremely strained. The 'ulama' were divided into two warring cliques. The tone of the debates degenerated. Leaving aside the Sunni and the Shia, the Hanafi and Shafi, the jurist and the philosophical differences, the very fundamentals began to be attacked. They would declare each other heretical. One would try his best to slight the other. Personal animosities had entered intellectual discussions. Pamphleteering began. Makhdum wrote to show that Abd-un-Nabi's sentence against Khizr Khan Shirwani and Mir Habash was sheer injustice and that he was legally unfit to lead prayers. Abd-un-Nabi wrote an equally 'tasteful' rejoinder.[60] Akbar was disgusted with both the parties.[61]

The Real Meanings of the Secrets

In compassing the downfall of Abd-un-Nabi and Makhdum-ul-Mulk Shaikh Mubarak and Abu-l-Fazl went astray. To discredit individuals, they discredited the system for which they stood—the system in which the words of the Quran are taken as they stand, in which there is no reading between the lines. To bring down the crows in the branches, they struck at the root of the tree.

They had already been jointed in their work by kindred spirits from Persia. In 1575 Hakim Abu-l-Fath and his younger brother came from Gilan and entered the Emperor's service. Soon their charming manners had won his heart.[62] Next year Mir Sharif of Amul came to Malwa from the Deccan and was invited by the Emperor, who happened to be there at this time, to have a parley with him. The Emperor liked his philosophical talks so much that he was taken into the court.[63]

In fighting against Abd-un-Nabi, Makhdum-ul-Mulk and other 'ulama', in addition to ordinary argumentation, interpretation and quotation, they took another line: the line of the 'real meaning' behind the ordinary. Simple words of the Quran, understandable by every man in the streets of Mecca or Medina and every beduin of the Arbian desert, were given far-fetched interpretations and named the 'real meanings'. The explanation of the Quranic injunctions in the mouth of Abu-ul-Fazl or Shaikh Mubarak were thus just what they or Akbar wanted them to be. The 'ulama' were not prepared to debate on these lines. They damned this process.

It was not something new. It was old poison in old bottles. The Hashimite movement against the Umayyads just before its final stroke and success turned out to be the Abbasid enterprise and the Abbasids came into power. The Alids were set aside and soon they began to organise a movement on the same lines and similarly underground. But the same cause of upholding the religion for which they had fought in the first instance was not forthcoming, because it was being championed by the Abbasids on the throne. It was to provide this missing central motivating lever that 'the real meanings' or 'the secrets'[64] were invented to make out 'the religion' (to be championed) by the political adventurers like Ubaid-Allah, the founder of the Ismaili or Fatimid rule in Tunis and Egypt; Qaramat and his followers, another turbulent element in Syria, Arabia and Messopotamia; and Hasan bin Sabah, who organised the Batiniyah[65] and was able to carve out a kingdom for himself. Abu-l-Fazl entered the Emperor's court with 'the candle of Sabahism in his hand and set the world on fire.'[66]

The Imam?

The Prophet of Islam was the spiritual as well as the corporal head of the Islamic polity. His successors were called the Khalifa (caliph) or the Amir-ul-Muminin. They were political as well as religious heads of the State. They were simply deputies (khalifas) of the Prophet, deputed to carry on his work of governing the state according to the Quranic Law, having, of course, the final right to interpret the law, adopt one of the various interpretations of a legal point and deduce new laws. They claimed no supernatural powers, no revelation, no infallibility, no airs of prophethood. They were elected by the people and claimed no Divine Right of Kingship. Such were the first five Caliphs (fifth Hasan, not Muawiya). The Abbasids tried to appear like them, although they reduced election to a farce and 'to be chosen by the people' was given semidivinity.

The Abbasid Caliph was the living successor of the Prophet, the living religious and political head of the people. When the Alid movement was organised to subvert the Abbasid power, first of all his position as the successor of the Prophet and religious and political head of the Muslims was rejected and the Head of the Movement was declared to be the real living successor of the Prophet, the real living spiritual and corporal leader of the Muslims. He was called 'the Imam.' He was the living spiritual head. His followers'first duty was to work and fight to make him the political head as well. The political power in the hands of the Abbasid usurper was to be restored to the real successor of the Prophet.

But the arduous and subtle task of the Imam required him to become something more than a Caliph. The head of an underground revolutionary political movement had to fight with weapons fair and foul. He required blind followers with the conviction that they were fighting for the Heavenly cause, under Heavenly guidance. The Imam, therefore, claimed supernatural powers and assumed the airs of prophethood. He was declared to be infallible.[67] He claimed the knowledge of 'the secrets'—the secrets which were known to no other person except 'the Imam of the Age'. And these 'secrets' or 'the real meanings' were the new interpretations of the Quranic texts to serve every fair or foul purpose of the Imam. If the revelation was to give a new knowledge, new laws and new moral values, these 'secrets' were equally potential and were used most unscrupulously. One can only wonder how a religion was being distorted and the religious sentiment of mankind being exploited to serve political ends.

Separation of the Law and the Executive

The Abbasid Caliph at Baghdad was the religious as well as the political head of the empire. But the governors he appointed in the provinces, in spite of exercising ample judicial powers, were not also religious heads in their jurisdictions. It were the Provincial Qazis appointed by the Caliph who were in charge of law and justice and the rest of the religious affairs in the provinces. When the provinces became independent, there and in other kingdoms set up later by various men of action, who even adopted the title of Sultan, this separation of the law and the executive continued. Hence the Sultan and the Qazi-ul-Quzzat under the Sultanate of Delhi and now against Akbar was installed his Sadr, Shaikh Abd-un-Nabi.

Position in India

Under the Sultans of Delhi, Babur or Humayun, the king was the political head of the state. He exercised absolute power;

he was the executive head of the civil government and commander-in-chief of the forces. To declare war or to make peace was his domain. He enforced law in the country. But he himself was not the law-maker. The Islamic law in its fundamentals was already there and deductive and inductive corollaries were the work of the religious Head of the state. This Religious Head of the state, called Sadr under the Mughuls, was appointed by the king himself. He used to be a scholar well-versed in various Islamic studies, particularly jurisprudence, and known for his piety. Once appointed to the post, he would become a rival power, against whom the king himself became helpless sometimes, because he stood for Islam. Any infringement of his ruling was considered the infringement of Islam and hence the infringement of the rights of all the Muslims, including commanders and soldiers, governors and administrators, officers and officials. Not his person but his office was important. While he was in office, kings had to respect him. He was thus the highest legal authority in the country. His ruling was final. He was not only an authority on paper. He was the actual Head of the Judicial organisation of the realm. All the Qazis or Judges in the country were under him. Moreover, he was in charge of all the endowment lands and stipends, primarily meant for educational purposes, throughout the empire. These lands were rent-free and he could distribute them at his free will. Such was this dual-system. But the mutual tug-of-war did not exist as long as the king did not want to enforce some law contrary to Islam. Due to the religious authority and the unbounded patronage in his hands, the Sadr enjoyed vast power.[68]

Shaikh Mubarak's Plan

Shaikh Abd-un-Nabi's powers were absolute. Even Akbar was afraid of interfering with him. Those who suffered at his hands, therefore, suffered because of his powers. But originally they belonged to the political ruler. If Akbar re-assumed Sadr's powers, the downfall of Shaikh Abd-un-Nabi would be complete. That was what Shaikh Mubarak wished in his heart of hearts.[69]

For cursing or reviling publicly anyone of the first three Caliphs, the Prophet's Wives or his Companions, punishment for a Shia from the Ecclesiastical Court of Abd-un-Nabi was death straightway. If Akbar stripped him of his powers, they would also be free. Hence they had joined hands with Shaikh Mubarak and Abu-l-Fazl. Hakim Abu-l-Fath, Hakim Humam, Sharif Amuli, Khanjahan who scandalized Makhdum, were all Shias.

Mahdi, a child of four or five, a descendant of Ali, one day went out and never returned. Ubaid-Allah, the founder of the Fatimid dominion, declared that Imam Mahdi would soon appear to lead the Muslims. Later the legend of the appearance of Imam Mahdi to renovate the Muslim world grew up. The Mahdist movement in India under the Surs was different from such movements in Tunis, Egypt, Syria, Iraq or Persia. But the background was the same. Ismaili propaganda was once briskly carried out in Sind, Multan and Gujarat. Before Mahmud of Ghazna came to India, Ismailis had already carved out the kingdom of Multan for themselves. Shaikh Mubarak might not have been a Mahdist, but his son's mode of discussion in the Ibadatkhana and their scheme for Akbar's Imamate were Mahdist *i.e.*, practically Ismaili. The Spiritual Lord with huge miraculous powers and supernatural abounding knowledge that Abu-l-Fazl makes out of Akbar is undoubtedly on the pattern of an Ismaili Imam. Every page of *Akbarnama* bears testimony to this. The 'ulama', the nobles and the rest all are dubbed as 'the worshippers of the outward form'. Only Akbar is 'the Lord of Meanings'. Shaikh Abd-un-Nabi, Mukhdum-ul-Mulk and the rest of the 'ulama' who unanimously condemned Shaikh Mubarak as 'the Mahdist', 'the misled and *the misleading*'[70] were not very far from the truth. The fact is that Shaikh Mubarak knew the world of Muslim ideas and was prepared to use any weapon ready to his hand. He wished Akbar to declare himself 'the Imam of the Age'.

Akbar's Belief that he had Supernatural Powers

Akbar's own religious life and mental working had also been heading towards religious leadership. If someone leads a religious life, people around tend to respect him. If he is a rich man or some high official, this respect tends to increase tenfold. If he becomes lowly with the lowly, they begin to revere him. But if a great king happens to be so, his subjects cannot help tendering their intense reverence. Akbar's religious life, his long hours of worship; his public marches from Agra to Ajmer, from Ajmer to Delhi, through Rajputana to Pakpattan, down from Lahore to Ajmer to proffer his supplications at the tombs of saints; and his walks on foot in honour of the Khwaja whenever approaching Ajmer;—had captured the public imagination. At the tombs he would sit down with the people, rich or poor, sometimes even on a platform of bricks. Akbar was not affecting religiosity. He was sincere. It was natural with him. His court musicians would sing devotional music. Books of similar contents were read out to him by his official reader. While he listened to them, his heart would melt and tears rush into his eyes.[71]

The people loved him, revered him, they had begun to look upon him as a great saint. They would attribute supernatural powers to the Emperor. These suggestions leading to auto-suggestion had their share in moulding the mental make up of the Emperor. He began to think himself not only favoured with the Special Favours of God, but also invested with Supernatural Powers. Soon belief in his supernatural powers had become general.

Muzaffar Khan was fighting against Afghans in Bihar in 1575. He was encamped beside a stream. With a small party he went out to gauge the depth of water and find out some suitable point for fording the river. About two hundred Afghans appeared on the opposite bank. Muzaffar ordered his men to cross the stream and fight them. Soon he himself followed them. The enemy fled, but the Afghan reinforcement reached them and they returned to give battle. The Imperialists were completely defeated and continued fleeing towards hills with Afghans at their heels till dusk deepened and gave them respite for the night. A man had been sent to hasten this way the main army on the other side of the river. But Muzaffar was utterly hopeless of their rescue. One of his men, Shaikh Jamal, had fallen on the ground where the action took place and become unconscious. After having regained his senses, he brought to Muzaffar the happy prophecy of their victory over the Afghans. He said, 'While I was lying unconscious I saw our Emperor fighting on the battlefield.' Soon after the main army arrived and the Afghans were defeated.[72]

Mihtar Saadat Peshrau Khan, another official, tells his story like this. "Raja Gajpati rebelled in Bihar. I fell a prisoner in his hands. Shahbaz Khan was sent against him. On the night Gajpati attacked the Imperialists, he ordered the execution of prisoners. Everyone of about seventy prisoners was entrusted to a soldier for this job. My executioner took me to a wood nearby. I sat down and in my last moments closing my eyes thought of my God and sought His grace in the name of my Saint Emperor. The sword did not descend upon my neck. After some time when I opened my eyes and looked up, my executioner approached me, full of awe and respect. He told me that he had tried his best to behead me, but his arm would not obey. Gajpati appointed another man to behead me. Thinking of my Emperor I again turned to my God. This sturdy man also could not discharge his duty. Gajpati was much annoyed. The night attack had not proved a success and he was fleeing before Shahbaz's soldiers. He ordered my executioner to take me with him on his elephant. The elephant on which we rode proved a vicious beast. The man in charge of me jumped down on the ground to escape his fury. This frightened the elephant and the beast took to flight. He was trumpeting aloud, Hearing his fearsome uproar all of the elephants ran off in different directions. My elephant was running swiftly. Shortly I found myself in the midst of a plain. I was in the 'haudah' behind the 'filban'. Both of my hands were tied at the wrists. I put them round the neck of the 'filban'. He considered I was holding him for support. Slowly but firmly I began to strangle him. As long as he was there I could not hope for my freedom. Soon the fact dawned upon the victim. He entreated for his life. I let him go and he descended down the elephant.

The elephant continued his flight till the day broke. When he stopped, I leapt down on the ground and became unconscious. When I awoke, it was midday. I sighted a soldier. Thank God! He proved a friend. Suddenly drums were beaten in the jungle—the Imperial drums!—to give direction to the lost. We headed towards the noise."[73] For Mihtar Saadat it was the supernatural power of the Emperor that had saved him from death.

In 1579 Sultan Khwaja returned from the Mecca pilgrimage and by relating the story of 'the spiritual help' of the Emperor throughout the voyage 'pleased the ears and hearts' of the people. On the outward voyage one night a child fell into the sea. The ship was speedily going ahead, but the crying of the child was approaching nearer and nearer. The Khwaja sent a rescuing party 'in the name of the Emperor.' The seamen considered it a vain toil. But at midnight they returned—with the child recovered alive! Everyone was convinced of the spiritual powers of the Saint Royal.[74]

Belief in Akbar's invincibility and supernatural powers had become so firm and wide-spread that it would lead others to prophesy about his power. When Shahbaz Khan captured Udaipur in 1578, a man had recently been put to death by the Rajput commandant of the fort. He was a Muslim hermit who had been living within the walls of the city fort for a long time and the people around used to seek his blessings. Three days before the surrender of the fort, early in the morning he came to the Rana's temple and standing aloft cried out the 'Azan'. The commandant of the fort was nonplussed. He inquired into his behaviour. The 'darvish' replied, 'Last night I have foreseen the conquest of this fort by the armies of King Akbar.' The commandant was infuriated and sentenced him to death. When this story reached Akbar, he thanked God for 'this special favour of His':[75] The saints of the age were foretelling his achievements.

When others were attributing such powers to him, Akbar also began to assume supernatural airs: foretelling the future, healing the sick and even trying to interfere with the natural elements. When he sent Sayyid Abd-Allah Khan towards Bengal, in 1576, to convey to the generals fighting there the news of the Rana's defeat, he added, 'As you go with the happy tidings of the victory in Mewar, you shall return with the good news of the conquest of Bengal.'[76] On his pilgrimage to Ajmer, in 1577, when an eye of Fath Khan Cheetabban was in pain, Akbar repeated some sacred text and blew upon his eye.[77] In 1578 rains were falling heavily. The people and the armies in distress petitioned their Saint Emperor. Akbar blew upon a mirror and placed it in the fire to stop the rain.[78]

Such was Akbar, the Chosen of the Lord, whom people had already accepted as saint, their 'Pir-o-Murshid', their Spiritual master, and who himself had begun to believe in his own supernatural powers, when Shaikh Mubarak to bring about the downfall of Abd-un-Nabi and Makhdum-ul-Mulk suggested to him to declare himself their Jurist Head as well, and become 'the Imam of the Age'.

Akbar also was tired of Abd-un-Nabi and Makhdum-ul-Mulk. Besides their religious pretensions and disgraceful mutual wrangles, in the administration of the Sadarat, of the Empire in the former's case and that of the Panjab in the latter's, they had proved inefficient and unreliable.[79] He desired to put an end to the rival jurisdiction of the Sadr,[80] to this state within the state. But there was one difficulty: he could not read or write efficiently. Among the events of 1578 we find recorded a significant event: 'Akbar began to take lessons in the elements of grammar from Shaikh Mubarak.'[81]

Shaikh Mubarak's Plan in practice

The first step towards the 'Imamat of the Age' was taken in 1579. Instead of the 'imam'[82] of the Cathedral Mosque of the capital Akbar decided to deliver the Friday sermon himself. The 'khutba' or the sermon to be delivered orally must have been the work of the Royal tutor. The opening verses were composed by his poet son, Faizi.[83]

But the maiden speech of even some of the most celebrated public speakers has not been a success. As soon as Akbar mounted the pulpit, he grew nervous and began to tremble. It was with difficulty that he could repeat the opening verses[84] and descending from the pulpit entrusted the 'imamat' to Hafiz Muhammad Amin Khatib.[85]

If Akbar had fared better in his first speech, it is likely that the later trend of his religious thought might have been very different. The atmosphere of the mosque and the responsibilities of the pulpit must have exercised their influence. It proved one of the most unfortunate failures of a maiden speech. Akbar never tried it again. The Emperor of Hindustan was not to cut a sorry figure amidst his subjects again. In a field where we fail we do not like our superiors. We befriend our inferiors in our field. Akbar could not like the cloquent speakers on the pulpit henceforth. He could not talk like a jurist scholar. He could talk like a mystic. Hence his aversion from the former and love of the latter.

Opposition to Abd-un-Nabi's powers and jurisdiction had been accumulating. Some of the provinces had already been put under Provincial Sadrs[86] directly under the Emperor. His own conduct and the interests of others had all contributed towards the same end. His power and his prestige both had suffered. The case of the Brahman of Mathura proved the last straw. His downfall came and with him fell the rival power of the Religious Head of the state.

Abd-ur-Rahim, the Qazi of Mathura, filed a case against a rich Brahman of that place in the court of the Sadr, Shaikh Abd-un-Nabi. The Qazi had collected building material to construct a mosque. The Brahman took it away and refused to give it back. In addition he insulted the Muslims and reviled the Prophet of Islam. Abd-un-Nabi summoned him to his court. He disobeyed.

Akbar sent Abu-l-Fazl and Birbar to bring him to the court. They brought him to the court and Abu-l-Fazl related what he had heard from the people at the spot. In conclusion he reported that the blasphemy of the Prophet by the Brahman 'was proven.' The Brahman was put into custody.

The jurists divided on the point of his punishment. According to some he was to be put to death. According to others he was to be flogged and disgraced in public. Abd-un-Nabi was for the death sentence.

Meanwhile the Rajput Queens, being approached or of their own accord, interceded in behalf of the Brahman and begged the Emperor for his life. Akbar was won over.

But Abd-un-Nabi wished to behead the Brahman. The Prophet reviled; the authority of the Sadr flouted; and everyone of the Hindu courtiers and all of his opponents trying to save the Brahman!—he issued the death warrant and the Brahman was beheaded.

Akbar heard of it and was infuriated. The Rajput Queens within and Hindu courtiers without were remarking. 'You patronize these Mullas and they don't care for you. To show their authority they put people to death without asking your permission.' They plied their remarks till the situation became intolerable for Akbar.

The Emperor placed this case before the jurists in the Ibadatkhanas. They had come to know the Royal wishes. All of them condemned Abd-un-Nabi.

The Emperor's anger was not satiated. Abd-un-Nabi ceased to attend the court. At this time Shaikh Mubarak paid a visit to the Emperor. Akbar referred the case of the Brahman to him. He said,

'You are yourself the Imam of the Age. In the promulgation of the religious and political regulations what need have you to refer to these people? They have not knowledge, but only unfounded fame for Knowledge.'

The Emperor replied,

'My dear teacher! Then why don't you set me free from the meshes of these mullas?'[87]

The Shaikh said,

'Claim the position of the Highest Mujtahid and ask them to sign a Document to confirm it.'

Shaikh Mubarak himself drafted this Document. His dream, cherished so long, was near materialization: Akbar was going to become the Imam; Abd-un-Nabi would be reduced to dust. The hour of vengeance had come.[88]

The Document[89] read—

"Whereas Hindustan has become the home of security and peace, justice and beneficence, and a large number of people, especially 'ulama' and 'fuzala', (of various religious views) from all the countries of Arab and Ajam have immigrated and adopted this land, We, all the principal 'ulama', who are well acquainted with the fundamentals and their corollaries, well-versed in the rational and traditional learning, and do justice to the requirements of religion, honest play and security, having duly considered the meaning of the Quranic injunction,

'Obey God, obey the Prophet and obey those who have authority among you.'

and the Ahadis,

'Surely the man who is dearest to God on the Day of Judgement is the Imam-i-Aadil, the Just Ruler.'

and

'Whosoever obeys the Amir obeys Me, whosoever rebels against the Amir rebels against Me.'

and having weighed other arguments, rational and traditional, give the ruling that

> the position of the Sultan-i-Aadil, the Just Ruler, is higher in the eyes of God than that of a 'mujtahid'[90];

and declare that

> the Sultan-ul-Islam, the Amir-ul-Muminin, Abu-l- Fath Jalal-ud-Din Muhammad Akbar Padshah Ghazi is the wisest, the most coversant with God and the most Just Ruler;
>
> hence, if there are more than one interpretations of a religious point by the 'mujtahids' in future, the interpretation adopted by the Emperor, for the political well-being of the country and economic good of the people, will be accepted unanimously and will be binding on all the subjects;
>
> and
>
> should the Emperor issue some new order that does not conflict with some Quranic injunction and is for the welfare of the people, it shall be binding on everyone; its opposition shall lead to loss in this world and damnation in the next.

This Documents has been written with honest intentions, beseeching the favour of God, and for the declaration and establishment of the rights of Islam, and is signed by us, the principal 'ulama' and the 'fuqaha',[91] in the month of Rajab, in the year, 987 A.H."[92]

Abd-un-Nabi and Makhdum-ul-Mulk were called in and

they had to sign the death-warrant of their authority with their own hands. It was also signed by many other 'ulama' like Qazi Jalal-ud-Din Multani, Sadrjahan Mufti, Ghazi Khan Badakhshi and others, all in the Emperor's pay, and Shaikh Mubarak. With what a gleeful heart he would have signed it![93]

The stray remarks and sullen resentfulness of religious dignitaries, who commanded vast respect, like Abd-un-Nabi and Makhdum-ul-Mulk, especially in a public place like a mosque, were dangerous.[94] Soon Akbar exiled them to Mecca. Shaikh Mubarak's triumph was complete.

NOTES

1. *Akbarnama*, ii, 60-61.
2. Ibid, 62.
3. Ibid, 32, 70-71.
4. *Akbarnama*,ii, 143
5. Ibid, 150-52.
6. Ibid, 154-55.
7. *Akbarnama*, ii, 162-65.
8. *Akbarnama*, ii,174-76.
9. Ibid, 201-2.
10. *Akbarnama*, ii, 285, 288-90.
11. Ibid, 286.
12. Ibid, 291.
13. Ibid, 292.
14. *Akbarnama*, ii, 319.
15. Ibid, 373.
16. Ibid, 372.
    Akbarnama, iii, 12.
17. *Akbarnama*, iii, 12.
18. Shabkhun: night attack.
19. *Akbarnama*, iii, 13-14.
20. Ibid, 15.
21. Ibid, 16.
22. *Akbarnama*, iii, 43-44.
23. Ibid, 44-45.
24. Ibid, 45.
25. *Akbarnama*, iii, 52.
26. Ibid, 52-53.
27. Ibid, 53.
28. Ibid, 55.

29. Ibid, 56-57.
30. *Akbarnama*, iii, 59-61.
31. Ibid, 61.
32. Ibid, 97.
33. Ibid, 100-1.
34. Alim: scholar well-versed in Islamic learning.
35. *Muntakhab*, ii, 172-73.
36. Hence the name the House of Worship i.e. the Ibadatkhana for the House of Discussions.
37. *Muntakhab*, ii, 202.
38. Ibid, 202.
39. Ibid, 207.
40. The permissible number.
41. *Muntakhab*, ii, 208.
42. *Muntakhab* ii, 208-9.
43. Ibid, 209.
44. Ibid, 209-10.
45. *Muntakhab*, ii, 210 وَلَذکرُ الله اَکبَر
46. The seal of Sultan Mahmud of Ghazna did not bear his name, Mahmud, meaning 'the Praiseworthy', but the words, 'Huwalmahmud', which mean 'Only He (God) is worthy of all praise.'
47. *Muntakhab*, ii, 210.
48. He had seen good days. He enjoyed Humayun's confidence. Sher Shah respected him. He was influential during the reign of Salim Shah. After the death of Salim Shah he invited Humayun to invade India. He did not invite him in words, written or oral. Detection would have meant his destruction. He sent Humayun a pair of shoes and a whip through a trader. They were to convey the message: Put on the shoes and whip your horse to invade India.

    Humayun gave him the title of Makhdum-ul-Mulk. He was called Shaikh-ul-Islam. He was a jurist and a scholar and had amassed wealth under many regimes. (Azad, *Darbar-i-Akbari*, p. 312). He was not a saint and he never claimed to have renounced the world.
49. *Muntakhab*, ii, 151.
50. *Muntakhab*, ii, 203.
51. Ibid, 203.
52. *Muntakhab*, ii, 204-6.
53. Ibid, 205.
54. Ibid, ii, 198.
55. *Muntakhab*, ii, 198.

56. Ibid, 208.
57. Shaikh Mubarak was a great scholar, well-versed in various branches of Islamic learning. He was much interested in Sufistic theology. This led to his interest in the Mahdist philosophical speculations. On this ground Abd-un-Nabi and Makhdum-ul-Mulk condemned him as heretic. After having squeezed a reluctant consent from Akbar, they issued orders for his arrest. The old man was lucky to get information in time. When the Muhtasib reached his house, he had, along with his sons, fled away and concealed himself. With the messengers of death following them at every turn, in one guise or another, the helpless fugitives journeyed from place to place and had to hid indoors whenever in a town. They begged the help of Salim Chishti in vain. Their miserable days prolonged. At last Mirza Aziz Kuka came to their rescue. He talked to the Emperor in their behalf and they were saved. All the time the womenfolk and children remained at home with no man to attend to their needs and tortured by suspense and lingering hope. The sorrowful story, with all its tragic details Abu-l-Fazl tells us in *Akbarnama.* Even when Akbar, having heard of the capabilities of Faizi as a poet, sent messengers, while besieging Chitor, to escort him to the court, it was with tearful eyes that his mother bade him good-bye and Shaikh Mubarak 'entrusted him to the protection of God.' (*Muntakhab,* ii,198-99, *Akbarnama,* ii, 304).
58. *Muntakhab,* ii 198-99.
59. Ibid, 211.
60. Ibid, 255.
61. Ibid, 259.
62. *Muntakhab,* ii, 211.
63. Ibid, 245-48.
64. باطن – اسرار
65. Batiniyah: followers of the 'Batin' i.e. the inside: the real meanings, the secrets.
66. *Muntakhab,* ii, 198. چراغِ صباحیان روشن گردانیده آتش در جهان انداخته ...
67. امام معصوم
68. To complete the outline of organisation of the Muslim state in India before Akbar, it may be added that the government of the state, civil and military, was exclusively in Muslim hands, except the non-muslims employed in the lower ranks of the revenue department. Non-muslims had to pay one extra tax, Jizya, in return for which they were exempt from military service and were free from religious persecution. They were not free in one

respect. Blasphemy against the Prophet of Islam, his Companions or his relatives was punishable with death.

69. *Muntakhab*, ii, 272.
70. *Muntakhab*, ii, 198-99.
71. *Akbarnama*, iii, 89.
    Muntakhab, ii, 228-29.
72. *Akbarnama*, iii,137-39.
73. *Akbarnama*, iii, 186-88.
74. *Akbarnama*, iii, 263.
75. Ibid, 239.
76. *Akbarnama*, iii, 176.
77. Ibid, 212.
78. Ibid, 239.
79. *Muntakhab*, ii, 204-6, 203-4.
80. Ibid, 268.
81. *Muntakhab*, ii, 265.
82. Imam: priest in a mosque.
83. *Akbarnama*, iii, 270-71.
    Tabaqat, ii, 343-44.
    Muntakhab, ii, 268.
84. خداوند که ما را خسروی داد — دل دانا و بازوی قوی داد
    بعدل و داد ما را رهنمون کرد — بجز عدل از خیال ما برون [کرده]
    بُود وصفش [زهد] فهم برتر — تعالی شـــانُه الله اکبر
    Muntakhab, ii, 268
85. *Muntakhab*, ii, 268.
86. *Akbarnama*, iii, 234.
87. *Muntakhab*, iii, 83 «چرا ما را از منت این ملایان خلاص نمی سازید؟»
88. *Muntakhab*, iii, 80-83; ii, 271-72 □
    او (شیخ مبارک) کمرِ جد و اجتهاد بسر میان «حقد و عناد» بسته گفت: «دعوی اجتهاد فرمائید
    و از ایشان محضری بطلبید»
    Muntakhab, iii, 83
89. The so-called Infallibility Decree.
    Mujtahid: Ecclesiastical and legal expert authorised to deduce corrollaries and give rulings.
90. Fuqaha: jurists.
91. *Muntakhab*, ii, 271-72.
    Tabaqat, ii, 345-46.
    Akbarnama, iii, 269-70.
92. *Muntakhab*, ii, 270-272.
    Tabaqat, ii, 344-45.
    Akbarnama, iii, 270.
    و شیخ مبارک بطوع در ذیل آن نوشت که این امری است که من بجان
    و دل خواهان و از سالها باز منتظر آن بودم
    Muntakhab,ii,272
93. *Darbar-i- Akbari*, 311, 316, 324.

NOTE A

Persian text of the so-called Infallibility Decree

محضر

مقصود از تشئید این مبانی و تمهید این معانی آنکه چون هندوستان صینت عن الحدثان بمیامن معدلت سلطانی و تربیت جهانبانی مرکز امن و امان و دائره «عدل و احسان شده» طوائف انام از خواص و عوام خصوصاً علمای عرفان شعار و فضلای دقائق آثار، که هادیان بادیه نجات و سالکان مسالک أُوتُواالْعِلْمَ دَرَجات اند، از عرب و عجم رو بدین دیار نهاده توطن اختیار نمودند،

جمهور علمای فحول، که جامع فروع و اصول و حاوی معقول و منقول‌اند و بدین و دیانت و صیانت انصاف دارند، بعد از تدبیر وافی و تامل کافی در غوامض معانی آیه کریمهَ اطیعُواالله وَ أَطیعُوا الرَّسُولَ وَ اوُلِی الْاَمْرِ مِنْکم

و احادیث صحیح

اِنَّ اَحَبَّ النّاسِ اِلیَ الله یَوْمَ الْقِیامَۀِ امامٌ عادلٌ

و مَنْ یُطِعِ الْاَمیرَ فَقَدْ اَطاعَنی وَ مَنْ یُعْصِ الْاَمیْرَ فَقَد عَصانی

و غیر ذالک من الشواهد العقلیه والدلائل النقلیه،

قرار داده حکم نمودند که

مرتبۀ سلطان عادل عندالله زیاده از مرتبۀ مجتهد است

و حضرت سلطان الاسلام کهف الانام امیرالمومنین ظِلَّ الله عَلَی الْعالَمین ابوالفتح جلال‌الدین محمد اکبر بادشاه غازی خَلَّدَاللهُ مُلْکَهُ اَبَداً اعدل و اعقل و اعلم باللهاند،

The Religious Headship

بنابران اگر در مسائل دین، که بین المجتهدین مختلف فیها است، بذهن ثاقب و فکر صائب خود یک جانب را از اختلاف، بجهت تسهیل معیشت بنی آدم و مصلحت انتظام عالم، اختیار نموده بآن جانب حکم فرمایند متفق علیه می شود و اتباع آن بر عموم برایا و کافه رعایا لازم و متحتم است،

و ایضاً اگر بموجب رای صوابنمای خود حکمی را از احکام قرار دهند، که مخالف نصی نباشد و سبب ترفیه عالمیان بوده باشد، عمل بران نمودن بر همه کس لازم و متحتم است و مخالفت آن موجب سخط اُخروی و خسران دینی و دنیوی است.

و این مسطور صدق وفور حسبةً للّٰه و اظهاراً لاجْراءِ حُقُوقِ الْاسْلام بمحضر علمای دین وفقهای مهتدین تحریر یافت و کان خالک فی شهر رجب سنه سبع و ثمانین و تسعمایه (۹۸۷)

منتخب التواریخ - ج ۲- ص ۲۷۱

The Fire-Blast

Chapter III

The Insurrection

Shaikh Mubarak and Abu-l-Fazal desired Akbar to become political as well as religious head of the state. Thereby they expected the ruin of their old enemies and security from persecution for themselves and others like them.

In Islamic polity the head of the state is also the religious head. Their plan was not, therefore, something alien to Islam. But they could not declare him Caliph in public. The Sunni world had accepted the Ottoman Sultan of Turkey as their Caliph.[1] And most of Akbar's nobles—Turkish, Mongol, Indian—the dominant percentage of his Muslim armies—mostly manned from Central Asia—and the majority of his Indian Muslim subjects were all Sunnis. Neither was there any question of Akbar's authority deriving from the Ottoman Caliph. Sultan Bayazid was defeated and imprisoned by Amir Timur. The Mughuls would always look down upon the Ottomans.

The only alternative left to Shaikh Mubarak and Abu-l-Fazl, therefore, was to give him the title of 'Imam'.[2] For the Sunnis it could have the meaning of just a head of a state, without any reference to the caliphate. But they themselves were making him out to be 'the Imam of the time'[3] on Ismaili lines: the Caliph, more than a Caliph: 'the Lord of Mysteries.'

The Document conferring the highest legal authority upon Akbar was very cunningly drafted by Shaikh Mubarak. The word Caliph is omitted. The word Imam is used, giving also the meaning of just a head of a state. And when the title Amir-ul-Muminin, an epithet of the Caliph, is used, it occurs after two other titles given to Akbar and thus is somewhat concealed, though it still stands there.[4] The first title given to Akbar is that of Sultan which was quite ordinary. The careful brief wording is placed in such a way that no objection could be made by the 'ulama'. On paper not much is claimed for Akbar. But in practice it meant absolute religious power.

And if Akbar was illiterate and unable to interpret the Quranic law, Shaikh Mubarak and Abu-l-Fazl were there to do it for him. The desire for vengeance, the love of influence, power, fame and name, had all been working slowly though quite efficiently. But the weapons used in the warfare had spared nothing for the victors.

Abu-l-Fazl by himself and later along with others of the same stock, in the Ibadatkhana discussions, philosophized and rationalised every Islamic belief to show that their opponents were leading nowhere. What is Revelation? What is Prophethood? What are Miracles? What is Prayer? Why Fast? Such were the topics raised and Akbar was at loss to understand them. He was not one of the bookish scholars like Abu-l-Fazl and others for whom such questions and their ready-made answere existed for the sake of discussion only without any reference to their inner life. Akbar was not a pedant. He was practical, whether on the battle-field or in the domain of ideas. He would continue to worry over these problems long after the learned scholars, after their return home late in the evening, were enjoying sound slumber. "The pure soul searched after 'the Truth'; instead doubts grew in his mind and began to torment him."[5]

In fact Abu-l-Fazl and Shaikh Mubarak proved his worst enemies. His beliefs, his convictions were shaken to the foundation. He was adrift. He doubted Revelation, doubted Prophethood, doubted Miracles, doubted Prayer, doubted the value of fasting.[6] He would not play the Imam in the way Shaikh Mubarak and Abu-l-Fazl expected him to do. They would have liked him to become the High Priest in the pulpit.

But it was their own fault. They had applied the method of making a novice to the making of the Imam. An Ismaili 'dai' or missionary used to approach a would be victim and create similar doubts in his mind and then the victim was told that only the Imam of the Age knew those mysteries. And after his conversion it was intimated that he could be initiated into them only by stages. The poor fellow would wait and serve and die. But who was going to remove Akbar's doubts and initiate him into mysteries? He was not a common man to stand and serve. He was the Emperor of Hindustan. He wanted to hear whatever they had to say there and then. Shaikh Mubarak and Abu-l-Fazl had nothing firm to give him. He turned to others.

Akbar did not know 'the Truth'. He would not claim that he did. Because he had no motive to do that. The Imam claimed to know 'the real meaning behind the words', 'mysteries behind the outward forms', because he had to hoodwink thousands of simple souls to form his legions to fight and assassinate and die, serving his political ambitions. Akbar stood in need of no militant blind followers. His Empire had already been built by the honest strength of his own arms and the exertions of his generals, Muslims and Hindus, Sunnies and Shias, who had served him as their Emperor as diligently as any could do a 'Master of the Truth'.

The Imam was to be 'all-knowing', 'king of word and meaning', 'initiated to the Truth'. But Akbar would turn to others to learn the Truth—to Hindus, Parsis, Mashaikh, Rishis,[7] Faqirs, even to sundry obscure old men. He did not become the Imam after the heart of Shaikh Mubarak and Abu-l-Fazl, though they went on painting him in the desired colours with such poor apologies: the Lord of the Truth knows every thing, but he does not know that he knows everything; he tries to learn from others, because he wants to honour them; he is the 'Master of Meaning', but the blind form worshippers cannot see him. Such was the only way for them to justify the Emperor's beliefs and practices henceforth.

Akbar had married Rajput princesses. He had been in close contact with Hindus. Previously he had interested himself in their religion to satisfy his curiosity. Now he turned to it in search of 'the Truth'. Devi Brahman explained to the Emperor the mysteries of the Hindu religion. He talked of the sacred themes like the worship of sun and fire; Brahma, Mahadev and Vishnu; Krishna and Rama; and Durga Maha Maii. He explained the 'Karma' and 'the Punarjanam'—the reward and punishment of man's deeds through the transmigration of the soul.[8] A man is poor, sick, blind, crippled or unhappy otherwise, because he was sinful in his previous life. Another is rich, healthy, handsome, sound of limb and sight and happy, because he was virtuous in his previous life. A very simple explanation of the mysteries and injustices of life which the Aryan mind, Hindu or Greek, had invented very early. It was a superb consolation. Akbar began to believe in it. He was at a loss to understand the eternity of the soul after the death of the body and its reward and punishment except by means of the transmigration.[9]

The Parsi priest, Dastur Mihrji Rana from Vesari (Nusari), in Gujarat, was invited to the court to explain Zoroastrian mysteries to the Emperor.[10] Outward symbols were said to have spiritual effect. Akbar was not averse to trying them. He put on the sacred shirt and bound round his waist the sacred girdle.[11] Due respect was shown to fire—the Light of God. The Emperor ordered a perpetual fire in the Royal Place.[12]

Even when Akbar's religious beliefs as a Muslim were accepting these non-Muslim elements, some Muslim theologians of one or the other denomination continued to suggest to him that he was the contemporaneons Prophet. Shaikh Taj-ud-Din of Delhi visited the court and presented his thesis that 'the Perfect Man' or 'the Spiritual Lord of the Age' was His Majesty, and, therefore, because of the honour due to him, which was said to be the religious duty of every faithful, obeisance before the Emperor was permissible. To this end, he proposed 'the ground kissing mode of respect.'[13] In its performance one had to bow, to do 'sajdah' to the Emperor. And the 'sajdah' of a Muslim is due to none but God.

Another philosophical point was made by Shaikh Yaqub Kashmiri. He was actually quoting Hamdani. He said, " 'The Prophet was the Guide and Satan the Tempter. Prophethood and Satanhood both play a part in life.'[14] In the present age, Your Majesty represents the former (by implication)".

While the Emperor was being suggested airs of prophethood, court writers began to omit the customary respects paid to the Prophet of Islam (naat) in introducing their books. After the praise of God, they would begin the panegyric of the Emperor. Muslims throughout detested it.[15]

The most important religious dignitary and a power for many year, who commanded great respect in public, was Abd-un-Nabi. His and Makhdum's influence formed quite a deterrent. They were sure to object and interfere, and their voice carried weight with Muslims. At the most Makhdum was a lover of wealth. With Abd-un-Nabi even Badauni has not been able to find fault except that he became arrogant. They suffered for their convictions. They would break rather than bend, a characteristic of theirs which deserves respect. Akbar was afraid of them. But when they had been despatched to Mecca, he could feel at liberty to discuss and to do whatever he liked. Moreover, after the confirmation of the 'Document', he had also become the final authority in the interpretation of the Quran. Neither past authorities nor the present were to be referred to.[16] The Islamic beliefs and practices, as the people knew them, now Akbar began to deem 'unreal', as mimicing others.[17] He discarded the 'Namaz', the Islamic mode of worship.[18] At the time of his visit (the last of the series) to Ajmer, in 1579, the Emperor examined the beliefs of the people, who had gathered there to pay their homage to the Saint's tomb, especially regarding the Quran, the Revelation, and the Prophethood. He would not believe in angels, genii and miracles, the continuity of the Quran and its being the Speech of God. The Quran was said to be the creation of God.[19] The Emperor, well-trained in the Ismaili strain by Shaikh Mubarak, Abu-l-Fazl and Shias from Persia, would exclaim in derision:

> "Regarding 'the Truth', in the hands of the blind, there is nothing but the Book (the Quran) and a few old graves."
>
> "The graves do not speak, No one seeks 'the Secrets of the Quran.'"[20]

Whatever he himself had begun to believe formed 'the Secrets of the Quran'.

Repeatedly Muslim religious scholars had declared Akbar 'the Spritual Leader of the Age', 'the Deputy or the Khalifa of God for his time.' Now he also liked to be repeated the words: "There is no god but God, and Akbar is the Deputy of God."[21] The 'Kalima', or the Muslim Confession of Faith, runs, "There is no god but God, and Mushammad is the Prophet of God." The words, 'Deputy of God', when placed as above, therefore, give the meanings of a 'Prophet'. Hence they could not be repeated publicly. Their use was limited to only a few persons within the palace.[22] But the news spread and had its due effect.

The religious sentiments of the ulama had been sorely touched. But their pockets had not been touched so far. They were touched this year, 1579. Abd-un-Nabi had been very liberal in granting rent-free lands to the ulama. Akbar had appointed Qazi Ali Baghdadi the year before to look into these grants and reduce them in undeserving cases. This year he presented the holders of 1000 to100 bighas before the Emperor. Akbar reduced their holdings in most of the cases. This created great resentment among the ulama[23]—the possessors of he pulpit, the only public platform of the time.

Rebellion in Bihar

Akbar was a ruler of Muslims, at times somewhat dangerous subjects. They are enjoined to obey their ruler even if he is a nose-cut negro, but only if he rules acccording to the Law. Otherwise they are equally enjoined to rise in revolt against the government. And Islamic Law is not the monopoly of any Parliament, Privy Council, Supreme Court of Chief Justice. Every Muslim is free to study the Law and pass any ruling. It is not the man who speaks that matters. It is the purport of what he says that matters. Free election of the Caliph did not last long. But the Islamic democratic spirit of the individual bridled the Muslim caesars for centuries. Whosoever claimed to be their leader, religious or political, Muslims demanded that his life and conduct be regulated on Islamic ideals. This incessant daring criticism of rulers, leaders and reformers, though sometimes unreasonable, reactionary, destructive or foolish, is an astonishing fact in Muslim history. It testifies to the vigour of a living people.

In 1579, Mulla Muhammad Yazdi, a Shia alim, Qazi of Jaunpur, with that 'Red Book of Revolution', the Quran, in hand, enjoined the people to rise in revolt against such a heretic ruler as Akbar. And the nobles of Bihar, like Muhammad Masum

Kabuli, Arb Bahadur, Said Beg Bakhshi, Mir Muizz-ul-Mulk, Samanji Khan, Niyabat Khan, Saadat Ali, Haji Kolabi, Said Badakhshi, Bahadur Badakhshi, Darvish Ali Sanjar and others, actually did so.

They had been much molested by the Imperial officers in Bihar, like Mulla Tayyib and Rai Purushottam Bakhshi, regarding the arrears and the branding of the horses. But is was the Emperor's religous innovations and Mulla Muhammad Yazdi's 'fatwa' against the Emperor that determined them to revolt and gave point to the insurrection.[24]

Akbar was, anyhow, still preoccupied. Birbar explained to him the mysteries of sun-worship. It was the sun that was responsible for ripening cereals and fruit and the existence of verdure and light and life. It was worthy of all respect. One should, therefore, turn one's face, while praying, towards the direction from which it rises (the East) rather than towards that in which it sets (the West–the Kaba direction).[25] He also deified fire and water and certain trees and stones, and sanctified the cow and even its dunghill, and tilak, the sacred Hindu mark on the forehead, and Janev, the sacred thread round the waist and shoulder of a Hindu.[26]

Birbar's talk contributed to the deification of the sun and planets and sanctification of the solar New Year Day by the Emperor. Akbar began to wear clothes of different colours: each day the colour of the planet ruling that day. He also began to repeat the 'Gayatri', the Prayer to Sun, at midnight and daybreak.[27]

On the New Year Day, 1580, the Emperor publicly bowed before the Sun and did the same before the Fire. When the lights were lit in the evening, the courtiers had to stand in respect. On the occasion of the Festival of the Eighth Day after the Sun's entry into Virgo, he came into the court with 'tilak' on his forehead, and the Brahmans, with all ceremonies, tied 'Rakhi' on his wrist.[28] Under Birbar's influence now he began to dislike cow slaughter.[29] Such were the influences of Brahmans and Parsis on him.

But some Muslim theologians, especially Shias, were still active in their efforts at prophet-making. They declared that

His Majesty was undoubtedly 'the Lord of the Age', expected for centuries to appear and put an end to all the seventy-two religions of Muslims and Hindus.[30] Sharif Amuli in a treatise brought forward Mahmud Basakhwani's testimony to the appearance of 'the Terminator of the False'[31] in the year, 990 A.H. Khwaja Maulana Shirazi Jafardan brought from Mecca a treatise by several of the Shaikhs of that place in which was propounded the same thesis. They said that the age of the world, 7000 years, was approaching its end and it was, therefore, the time for the appearance of the expected Mahdi. He himself also wrote a treatise on this topic and presented it to the emperor. Similarly, other Shias quoted from Ali to the same effect. Some of them brought forward, to support their thesis, the following quatrain, said to be of Nasir Khusrau, the well-known Ismaili dai:

> In Nine eighty nine, by the Decree of the Heavenly Will,
> The stars will form such an array that
> In the year of Leo, in the month of Leo, on the day of Leo,
> The Lion of God will come forth from behind the Veil.[32]

And those who opposed these prophet-makers were not safe from the Royal wrath. Hakim-ul-Mulk dared to oppose them. He described Abu-l-Fazl (the Father of learning) as Fuzla (the rubbish). Akbar exiled him to Mecca.[33]

The same year the first Jesuit Mission from Goa arrived in the court and the Christian Father explained the riddle of the Holy Trinity. Prince Murad was entrusted to one of them for taking lessons in the Bible, Abu-l-Fazl was ordered to render the Bible into Persian. Akbar showed due respect not only to the Bible but also to the paintings of the Virgin and Christ. This respect was like image-worship, so strictly denounced in Islam.[34] To crown all, the Christian Saints proved the most foul-mouthed. They would talk of the 'hideous and heinous infernal monster Mohmet'[35] and prove him to be the Anti-Christ.[36]

Akbar had tried the patience of the Muslim 'umara' too much: their Prophet insulted; their religion insulted; their Book insulted; they themselves insulted. It reached the breaking point. They cursed Abu-l-Fazl and his colleagues; they cursed Birbar;[37] they crushed the Jesuits.

Revolt in Bengal

What was happening in the court was not limited to the court. The news spread in the Provinces. Bihar was already in arms. In Bengal Muzaffar Khan, the Imperial Governor, had been maltreating Turkman nobles regarding the arrears and the branding of horses. Now the news of the Neo- Islam from the court reached them.[38] They held a conclave and reached a unanimous decision. Under the Turkman general, Baba Khan Qaqshal, they rose in revolt.[39]

The Emperor's authority in Bihar had come to an end. The loyalists had been defeated and the imperial Bakhshi, Rai Purushottam, put to death.[40] Now there opened correspondence between Baba Khan and Masum Khan Kabuli, the rebel leader in Bihar. They came to an understanding and the Bihar forces joined the Turkmans in Bengal. The combined forces marched against Muzaffar Khan and besieged him in the fort of Tanda. The fort fell and he was put to death. The whole of Bengal and Bihar were in rebel hands.[41]

Under the richly decorated gorgeous 'Bargah', the tent audience avenue, made for presentation to Akbar, the rebel leaders met and declared Akbar's brother, Mirza Hakim, Emperor of Hindustan. He had already been invited to invade the country from the North-West in collaboration. In his absence Masum Khan Kabuli was made his 'Vakil' or the Vicegerent and was given the title of Khan-i-dauran. Baba Khan Qaqshal was appointed as Governor of Bengal and was entitled Khan Khanan, and Jabbari, his nephew, son of Majnun Khan, became Khanjahan and Panj Hazari. Wazir Jamil was awarded the title of Khanzaman and the office of Tuzak Begi. Khalidin was entitled as Azam Khan, Mirza Beg as Bahadur Khan and Jan Muhammad Behsudi as Khan-i-alam. Arb Bahadur, the other prominent rebel leader of Bihar, was awarded the title of Shujaat Khan.[42] Actual command lay in the hands of Masum Khan Kabuli and Baba Khan Qaqshal, but to grace their side with some person of Royal pretensions, they declared Mirza Sharf-ud-Din Husain, Akbar's son-in-law, as their supreme commander.[43]

Akbar meanwhile had sent Raja Todar Mal against the Bihar rebels and all the nobles still loyal in the East had been ordered to co-operate with him.[44] Masum Khan Farnakhudi, Governor of Jaunpur, joined him with his three thousand well-trained soldiers, but he seemed to be harbouring treason in his mind.[45] Humayun Farmuli, who had witnessed the Emperor examining the beliefs of Muslims at Ajmer and heared discourses on Neo-Islamics,[46] openly deserted the Raja and went over to the enemy. Turkman Divana also left with him.[47]

Everything was being reported to the Emperor. Akbar did not fail to realize the gravity of the situation.[48] Mirza Aziz Kuka had been stripped of his office, all of his ranks and honours and confined to his residence and garden, because he opposed the Branding Regulations, so dear to the Emperor. But his loyalty was above suspicion. Akbar now restored him to his previous position, appointed him as Governor of Bengal, awarded him the robes of honour and sent him to fight the rebels in the East.[49] Shahbaz Khan, the intrepid general fighting against the Rana, was also recalled from Mewar and despatched against them.[50]

Akbar's wrath now fell upon the priestly class. Mulla Muhammad Yazdi and Mir Muizz-ul-Mulk were sent for from Jaunpur. When they reached Firozabad, about fifty miles from Agra, they were ordered to be separated from their soldiers and carried to Gwalior, crossing the Jamna in boats. Soon afterwards another 'farman' arrived ordering their destruction. Hence the guards took seat in one boat and the two of them were seated in another. In the midst of the river 'the boat of their life was sunk amid the whirls of death.' Soon after Qazi Yaqub arrived from Bengal and was despatched 'to follow them'. One by one every one of the 'mullas' who were suspected of disloyalty were sent to the 'secret chamber of non-existence.'[51]

To break the influence of the 'ulama' at Lahore, they were spread out over the country. They were appointed at such far-flung places that they were virtually exiled. Qazi Sadr-ud-Din Lahori was appointed Qazi of Baraich in Gujarat. Mulla Abd-ul-Shakur was appointed Qazi to Jaunpur. Mulla Muhammad Masum was sent to Bihar. Shaikh Munavvar was appointed

Sadar of Malwa. Many others suffered the same fate. Haji Ibrahim Sarhindi was also sent away from the court to act as Sadr of Gujarat.[52]

Akbar also turned his attention towards the 'mashaikh.' He wanted to know if they and the 'ulama' were really what they were said to be, truly deserving of the rent-free state lands they were holding. Moreover, he had utterly lost faith in the pretensions of the mashaikh to guide others spiritually. He had tried them long and found them wanting. Still many of them had hundreds of disciples and thus exercised considerable influence. Akbar wanted to put an end to this public influence of theirs based upon unreality. He issued orders, therefore, to the 'ulama' and the 'mashaikh' throughout the country to present themselves in the court. The Emperor would himself interview everyone of them and settle the question of land according to qualifications. The lands were reduced in every case anyhow. But those of the mashaikh, or the so-called saints, who accepted disciples, organized music assemblies or showed some miraculous tricks, were straightway imprisoned in forts or exiled to Bengal or Bhakkar.[53]

But the Royal Saint himself was trying to secure the utmost loyalty and sincerity from his own disciples. When Akbar's life was intensely religious and in certain respects on the pattern of a saint, people had begun to accept him as their 'Pir-o-Murshid' (the Spritual Guide), take 'bait' (oath of spiritual allegiance) to him and become his 'murids' (disciples). Due to his present innovations his position as the Pir-o-Murshid dwindled among his courtiers. Those who accepted his new-fangled ideas were less than a dozen. The prominent among them at the time were Birbar and Abu-l-Fazl, a Brahman and a Mullah's son, who had no principle in life except to serve the man in power. In Abu-l-Fazl's attitude one easily discerns the cynical ' Yes, Sire' of a successful courtier. Such were the persons who still named themselves as the Shahinshah's murids and called him their Pir-o-Murshid. For them, this year, the Emperor Saint initiated Four Grades of Sincerity. Those who were prepared to spend their wealth in the service of their Spiritual Lord stood on the lowest rung. Next came those who would sacrifice their life also. Above them were those who would give their honour as well. On the highest stood those who would renounce not only their wealth, life and honour, but also their religion, explained as merely a particular outwards form.[54] The loyalty and sincerity were emphasised when they were needed most.

Akbar had sent three of his most prominent generals, one the most tactful, the second most loyal and the third most warlike, against the rebels in the East. But he himself would not leave the capital. He expected Hakim's invasion from he North-West.[55] He must be ready to march ahead and meet him in the Panjab rather than go to the East and leave the capital for the invader with all its prestige and treasures.

The rebellion in the East was not an ordinary one. Powerful nobles had rebelled throughout the Eastern provinces, championing the cause of religion and in the name of an equally respectable Royal scion. Treason was also simmering under the surface in the court, among the rank and file, throughout the masses. They were not sure about the consequences. Hence their apparent loyalty, in spite of their disloyal intentions. The whole of the personnel of the rival government had been set up in the East. The rebels had been and were in communication with the West—the Kabul Government. Raushan Beg had been sent from Kabul to instigate rebellion in Bengal.[56] Mulla Muhammad Yazdi, Qazi of Jaunpur, had given the 'fatwa' that to fight against Akbar had become the religous duty of every Muslim. Mir Muizz-ul-Mulk, another noble from the priestly class, was with him. Qazi, Yaqub, the Qazi of Bengal, once the Imperial Qazi, had joined them. Humayun Farmuli and Turkman Divana of the Imperial army, with their contingents, had openly deserted the loyalist Todar in the name of religion. The attitude of many others was clearly treasonable. The most prominent of them was the powerful Governor of Jaunpur, Masum Khan Farnakhudi, Mirza Ali Alamshahi, Mirki, Idi, Shahab Bakhshi and Kochak Yasaval were preparing to escape towards the East. Mir Ali Akbar helped them by conveying their mutual messages. His loose talk was also adding fuel to the fire.[57]

Akbar had been trying to pacify the public. On his return journey from his Ajmer visit in the previous year he had ordered a tent-mosque to accompany the royal entourage, where he would duly say five prayers publicly everyday.[58] This year Prince Danyal was sent to pay respect at the Ajmer tomb and was given five thousand rupees to be distributed among the people at that place.[59]

Not only had Shahbaz been recalled from his command against the Rana, ceasing successful operations in that quarter, but generals of Malwa and Gujarat had also been ordered to end hostilities in the Deccan and await orders. One of them, Shujaat Khan, Governor of Malwa, was actually sent for.[60] Such was the gravity of the situation.

Conspiracy at the Court

In the very midst of fighting against the rebels, Khwaja Shah Mansur, the Imperial Finance Minister, demanded arrears in the severest terms from Tarsun Muhammad Khan and Masum Khan Farnakhudi. The latter's loyalty had already been wavering. Tarsun Muhammad Khan was the most important loyalist noble in the East, fighting for the Imperial cause. They were exasperated. Instead of receiving encouragement and reward for risking their lives on the battle-field and not joining the rebel cause, they were getting reprimands.[61] It was as if to drive them to the enemy ranks.

Shah Mansur's action at this particular juncture could have a motive. Abu-l-Fazl does not pursue the subject and leaves it after having made one interrogative remark: 'What should I call this demand? And belonging to which party should I consider the out-of-season demander?'[62] But this one remark provides us with a perspective peep into the situation. The existence of a disloyal party is clearly implied.

And Akbar did suspect his Finance Minister of belonging to that party. He was dismissed from office and sent to prison.[63]

The Emperor was in real distress these days, anxiously watching his court and wishfully awaiting news from the Western front. Sometime we find him excusing rebels for their conduct, because all was decreed and destined; sometime foretelling the destruction of the mischievous and reversion to loyalty of the virtuous.[64]

When the enemy raised the siege of Munger and fled away and the news reached the capital, the religious Emperor praised his God and thanked Him for His help with deep sincerity and utter humility. In the hour of his happiness he would praise and worship his Lord.[65]

But the rebellion was not yet over. Akbar took an oath promising his God that if the insurrection failed, he himself and his courtiers, in gratitude, would not kill certain animals for twelve years to come.[66]

In the beginning of 1581, Mirza Hakim was reported to have sent his vanguard under Shadman across the Indus. It was repulsed by Kunwar Man Singh, who had at once been ordered from Sialkot to march ahead and take charge of the frontier.

Akbar despatched Rai Rai Singh, Jagan Nath, Raja Gopal and others, with numerous war elephants, towards Lahore, but at the same time ordered the generals in charge of the frontier to let Mirza Hakim cross the Indus and enter the Panjab.[67]

The Emperor now prepared to meet his invading brother. The capital was entrusted to Sultan Khwaja, Shah Quli Mahram and Shaikh Ibrahim with Prince Danyal at their head. Accompanied by his two sons, Prince Salim and Prince Murad, and his forces that had received eight months' pay in advance,[68] he left Fathpur[69].

A few days later he was at Delhi. There he paid visit to his old gods, tombs of various saints,[70] more for the sake of his subjects perhaps.

Shah Mansur had been suspected of double-dealing and imprisoned. But soon, when his successor, Wazir Khan, had to be sent away as Governor of Avadh, he was restored to his previous position.[71]

Shadman, Mirza Hakim's general, was killed fighting against Man Singh. Among his private things there were found three letters from Mirza Hakim. Man Singh sent them to the Emperor. One of them was addressed to Khwaja Shah Mansur, in which his profession of loyalty and co-operation were acknowledged and he was promised due reward. Akbar considered it expedient to keep silent.[72]

When, on his march towards the Punjab, Akbar reached

Sonipat, Malik Sani,[73] Diwan of Mirza Hakim, reached the camp, quartered with Shah Mansur, sought service through him and gave out that he had suffered at the hands of the Mirza and had, hence, deserted him. But it was said to be simply a ruse; he was believed to have been sent to canvass among the courtiers and 'hasten the evil-doers in their scheme.'[74] Akbar imprisoned the Malik. Khwaja Mansur opposed it and there was raised an uproar. The Emperor's suspicions about the Khwaja were doubly supported. He sent him also to prison.[75]

A few days later another set of letters incriminating the Khwaja was brought to the Emperor. On this Akbar ordered Shah Mansur to provide sureties for his loyal conduct or suffer death 'to become an example for the short-sighted and the greedy and serve as an eye-opener for the vicious going astray.'[76] Shah Mansur could not provide sureties. The Emperor ordered him to be hanged from a tree, 'because the time was in chaos due to the weak-sighted and the base, and the moment was critical.'[77]

The letters which led to the destruction of Shah Mansur have been said to a forgery on the part of Karm-Allah and certain other nobles.[78] But the references to 'the evil-doers', 'the short-sighted and the greedy', 'the vicious going astray', 'the weak-sighted and the base', and to 'the chaos of time' and 'the critical moment' give out in unequivocal terms the existence of treason and conspiracy.

The second set of letters which brought about the death of Shah Mansur seems clearly the concoction of his enemies. Not only because they have been dubbed so by the trustworthy contemporary historians like Nizam-ud-Din Ahmad and Badauni, but also because of the way in which they were said to have fall into the hands of the Imperialists. Malik Ali brought these letters to the court and related that his men, returning from the Ludhiana ferry (which was under his supervision) met in an inn at Sarhind a courier whose feet had swollen. He told them that he was a servant of Shah Beg who was in the service of Khwaja Shah Mansur as 'shiqdar' of his jagir at Firozpur, thirty 'kurohs' from Lahore; that Shah Beg had sent those letters to Khwaja Shah Mansur through him, but, as his feet had swollen, he would be very thankful to them if they took charge of the letters and conveyed them to the addressee. Malik Ali told the Emperor that his men had brought home those letters and when they broke the seal,[79] the treasonable documents came to light.[80]

The whole story reads like an unconvincing piece of fiction. But to understand the political tension of the moment and the tension of Akbar's mind, one has to know that he did believe it and sentenced his Diwan to death.

Karm-Allah and his accomplices were shrewd enough to gauge the situation correctly and think of this fabrication to destroy the man they hated at this opportune moment.

Shah Mansur, however, had already provided ample ground for suspicion of his treason. The first set of letters cannot be so easily disposed of. It appears related to facts rather than fiction. Nizam-ud-Din Ahmad and Badauni both[81] declare that all the letter in both sets were forged. But it seems just a generalization of the whole matter, when actually only the second set proved a concoction later on. Moreover, they particularly emphasize the forgery of the second set.[82]

If the first set of letters was also a forgery, two problems remain unsolved. Firstly, the first set of letters was in the handwriting of Mirza Hakim's Secretary.[83] How did Karm-Allah establish contact with him? Was the Secretary also a traitor to his own master? Karm-Allah was a brother of Shahbaz Khan and belonged to the loyalist party in Hindustan. Why did the Secretary join hands with Karam-Allah to campass the death of Shah Mansur? Secondly, the letters in the first set were not all addressed to Shah Mansur. Two of the three were addressed to Qasim Khan Mir-i-Bahr and Hakim-ul-Mulk Gilani.[84] What motive had Karam-Allah and his friends to destroy them also? They had no grudge against them, so far as we can find in the historical record. On the other hand we know that Akbar had already exiled Hakim-ul-Mulk to Mecca, because he was opposing the Neo-Islamic regime,[85] and that later when Akbar invited him to come back, *he would not.*[86] And we also know that Qasim Khan was the younger brother of Khwajgi Muhammad Husain, 'one of the trusted nobles of Mirza Hakim.'[87]

Besides, Abu-l-Fazl's silence regarding the forgery or validity of the letters is significant and two of his remarks about Shah Mansur are revealing: 'Shah Mansur did not realise that in the short life *counterfeiting* has no permanence', and 'If he had some thankfulness towards his God, *some sincerity* (loyalty) *towards his King,* kindness towards the people and had not been so greedy (ambitious), strict and harmful, the wrath of the Emperor would not have fallen upon him.'[88]

I have discussed the question of Shah Mansur's treason in detail, because it proves the existence of a conspiracy in the court. There it was and the tension of the situation clearly comes out.

Invasion of the Panjab

Meanwhile Mirza Hakim, having crossed the Indus, had reached Lahore and besieged it. Said Khan, Raja Bhagwan Das and Kunwar Man Singh were within the city. They would not attack him as they were not allowed to do so. But they were vigilant in guarding the city and kept the 'big-turbaned nonsense-talkers of the city from communicating with the enemy outside.'[89] This casual half a sentence confirms the existence of a hostile priestly class at Lahore as well, who were opposed to Akbar and ready to welcome his brother; and their presence implies the existence of people under their influence.

From Sarhind Akbar issued orders to Provincial governors, 'shiqdars' and other administrative officials throughout his realm to prepare a record, village by village, of every man and his profession, and to see whether everyone followed some honest trade in earning his livelihood. They were to examine the means of income and to keep an eye upon the expenditure of every man. The motive behind this plan was to hunt down the priestly and the saintly persons who had influence upon the masses and were receiving money from them.[90]

But the champion of Akbar's opponents, Mirza Hakim, had already raised the siege of Lahore and was hurriedly fleeing back towards Kabul. The approach of the aweinspiring Maha Bali was too much for him.

From Sarhind to Kalanaur, crossing the Satluj near

Machhiwara, from Kalanaur, crossing the Ravi near that city, the Chanab near Ramgadh and the Jehlam near Rawalpindi, Akbar reached the bank of the Indus. It formed the North-Western frontier of his Empire and to forestall future trouble he had decided to strengthen this outline of defence by constructing here a strong fort and keeping a powerful garrison therein. This decision of Akbar also speaks of the seriousness of the situation felt before Hakim's invasion. With his own hands now he laid the foundation-stone and named the fort as Attock Banaras against another frontier fort in the extreme East named Cuttack Banaras.[91]

Akbar had determined to advise his brother after having entered his capital. 'Because a thousand pieces of advice from afar are not so effective as one to one's face.'[92] Hence he now decided to cross the Indus and march towards Kabul. The idea was, no doubt, to declare his complete triumph thus.

But his nobles did not wish to proceed to Kabul, some of them certainly because of their sympathies with Mirza Hakim.[93] Akbar asked Abu-l-Fazl to write down their opinions for him.[94]

Abul-l-Fazl fells us that they could not convince him of the wisdom of their decision, because 'he had no white hair and long beard and the cloak of hypocrite old age.'[95] He is here referring to some of the nobles and thus confirms the existence of some veteran nobles who were not loyal to the depths of their heart.

Akbar himself was hesitant to march upon Kabul, but on very different grounds. He did not want his brother to flee to Turan.[96] The tale of Akbar's apostasy from Islam had reached beyond the confines of his Empire. Turanis were very zealous in religious matter. A son of Humayun in the hands of a powerful monarch like Abd-Allah Khan Uzbek of Turan would have been a dangerous pawn on the chess-board of politics.

Akbar wanted Mirza Hakim to come to terms on the lines he had dictated. But in vain. To accomplish this, he must reach Kabul.

But he was not sure of the full co-operation of his generals. He earnestly desired to have their consent, or to know their opinions—to search their hearts, to discern their motives. Again they were asked to convene a conference and Abu-l-Fazl to record the minutes, but with no better results. Besides Abu-l-Fazl, their unanimous decision was to accept Mirza Hakim's terms and return to Hindustan. Akbar was much annoyed and prepared to go alone with the personal guard and the lascars. The umara had to follow him.[97]

The Emperor had already sent ahead a strong force with Man Singh, Mirza Yusuf Khan, Rai Rai Singh, Karm-Allah (the forger of the Shah Mansur case letters), Sayyid Hamid Bukhari, Makhsus Khan, Qalij Khan, Naurang Khan, Madhav Singh and others with Prince Murad at their head.[98] Mirza Hakim would not submit without fighting.

So common were the rumours about the defection of Akbar's nobles and forces that they were generally expected to change sides on the battlefield. Mirza Hakim considered as if all of them were worth-trying and threw his feelers before the battle. Letters were sent to Qalij Khan, Mirza Yusuf Khan, Naurang Khan, Ali Murad and some other leaders of the Chughtai clans, expecting betrayal and promising rewards. But Akbar had been very careful in selecting his advance army. Qasim Khan and the like had been left behind on the Indus bank. Mirza Yusuf Khan tore the letter into pieces and Ali Murad killed the letter-bearer.[99]

Mirza Hakim fought to his utmost and when defeated took shelter among the neighbouring hills. The resources of a small poor hilly tract were matched against the whole strength and vast wealth of Hindustan. The pick of Akbar's army and the best of his personal elephants had been sent in advance. He himself was coming behind with such seasoned generals as Zain Khan Kuka and Muttalib Khan, and the rest of the huge army was encamped beside the Indus.[100] Akbar had mobilized the biggest army he ever did throughout his long military career. Perhaps he wanted all his nobles, including the waverers, to remain directly under his eyes. Whatever the cause, it shows how serious he considered the danger of this insurrection.

But the danger was by now practically over. Akbar entered Kabul triumphantly. He tried his best to persuade Mirza Hakim to come to see him, but in vain, though he tendered his apologies, begged his forgiveness, proffered his allegiance and sent his son to pay homage to his uncle. Akbar pardoned him and restored his kingdom.[101] The subjugation of the insurrection from the West was complete. The Emperor now started on his return journey.

On the Indus bank Shaikh Farid arrived in the camp from Bihar with the tidings of the suppression of rebellion in the East. When the Emperor had crossed the Indus and entered Hindustan, Raja Todar Mal reached the court and repeated the happy news.

Akbar reached Delhi, visited the grave of his father, and stayed with the Queen Dowager, Haji Begum. In the evening he was informed that his mother, Queen Maryam-makani, had come out from the capital, Fathpur, to receive her son. The Emperor left Delhi and went ahead to receive his mother.

Akbar proceeded towards Fathpur, where the poet laureate was singing his 'Ode to the Emperor':

The lightsome breeze is blowing in Fathpur,
Because my Emperor approaches from afar.[102]

As there was little fierce fighting, this campaign of Akbar's may appear to us merely full of fury. But the contemporaries had a better appreciation. In their opinion it was one of the biggest rebellions in the history of India and Akbar suppressed it successfully.[103]

Shahbaz Khan had joined the court at Panipat with great pomp and show and paid his homage to the Emperor. After having completely suppressed rebellion in Bihar, he had returned to the capital, and during the interval, in the country from the confines of Bengal to the frontiers of the Panjab, had been behaving like an absolute monarch, bestowing jagirs and 'mansabs' of whatever magnitude he liked and upon whomsoever he liked, without any reference to the Emperor. When Akbar questioned his behaviour, he replied,

'Dear Emperor, if I had not rewarded them and patronized them in this way, they would have rebelled one and all. Now you have come.

Let them have whatever you like,
Get back whatever you like.

The soldier is yours,
The country is yours.'[104]

The Revolt was over.

NOTES

1. When Akbar canvassed Qutb-ud-Din Khan Atga about the Neo-Islam, he remarked, "What will the *Sulatan of Rum* (the Ottoman Caliph) and other kings say, when they hear about these things? whether formal or real they all confess the same Islam." (*Muntakhab*,ii, 274.)
2. *Akbarnama*, iii, 270 گیتی خدیو امامِ وقت و مجتهد روزگار است
3. *Akbarnama*, iii, 270.
4. حضرت سلطان الاسلام کهف الانام امیرالمومنین ظل الله علی العالمین ابوالفتح جلال الدین محمد اکبر بادشاه غازی خلدالله ملکه ابداً
   Muntakhab, ii, 271
5. شبهات باطله از کمین برآمده پادشاهی را که جوهری نفیس و طالب حق بود در شک انداخته حیرت بر حیرت افزود و مقصود از میان رفت
   Muntakhab, ii, 255
6. *Muntakhab*, ii, 211, 257, 273.
7. Mashaikh: Muslim saints.
   Rishis: Hindu saints.
8. *Muntakhab*, ii, 257-58.
9. Ibid, 273.
10. *Muntakhab*, ii, 261.
11. Smith, *Akbar, The Great Mogul*, 163.
12. *Muntakhab*, ii, 261.
13. Ibid, 259.
14. *Muntakhab*, ii, 259. زمین بوس
15. *Muntakhab*, ii, 269, 366.
16. Ibid, 272-73, 301
17. *Muntakhab*, ii, 272 اسلام را تقلید نامیدند
18. *Muntakhab*, ii, 275.
19. The Mutazilite doctrines.
20. از حقیقت بدست کوری چند مصحفی ماند و کهنه گوری
    چند گور با کس سخن نمی‌گوید «شرِ قرآن» کسی نمی‌جوید
    Muntakhab, ii, 273
21. *Muntakhab*, ii, 273 لا الله الا الله اکبر خلیفهٔ الله
22. *Muntakhab*, ii, 273.
23. Ibid, 274, 276.
24. *Muntakhab*, ii, 276, 281.
    Akbarnama iii, 284-85.
    Tabaqat, ii, 349-50.
25. *Muntakhab*, ii, 260.
26. *Muntakhab*, ii, 260.

27. Ibid, 260-61.
28. Ibid, 261-62.
29. Ibid, 260-61.
30. حالا صاحب زمانی که رافع خلاف و اختلاف هفتاد و دو ملت از مسلم و هندو باشد حضرت‌اند
    Muntakhab, ii, 287
31. بردارندهٔ باطل *Muntakhab*, ii, 287
32. در نهصد و هشتاد و نه از حکم قضا آیند کواکب از جوانب یکجا در سالِ اسد، ماه اسد، روزِ اسد، از پرده برون خرامد آن شیر خدا
    Muntakhab, ii, 287
33. *Muntakhab*, ii, 275, 285.
    Tabaqat,ii, 354.
    Akbarnama, iii, 317.
34. *Muntakhab*, ii, 211-12, 260.
35. Aquaviva's letter to the Rector of Goa, cited in Smith, *Akbar, The Great Mogul*, 175.
36. *Muntakhab*, ii, 260.
37. Ibid, 274.
38. *Akbarnama*, iii, 293.
    (The 9th cause of the Revolt in Bengal)
39. *Muntakhab*, ii, 280.
    Tabaqat, ii, 348-49.
    Akbarnama, iii, 290-91.
40. *Muntakhab*, ii, 281.
    Tabaqat, ii, 350.
    Akbarnama, iii, 287.
41. *Muntakhab*, ii, 281-82.
    Tabaqat, ii, 350-51.
    Akbarnama, iii, 301-4.
42. *Akbarnama*, iii, 304-5.
43. Ibid, 305.
    Tabaqat, ii, 351.
    Muntakhab, ii, 282.
44. *Akbarnama*, iii, 287.
45. Ibid, 306-7.
    Muntakhab, ii, 282.
    Tabaqat, ii, 351.
46. که در وقتِ گفتگوی مسلمانیهای جدید و تکلیف و امتحانِ مردم در اجمیر آن معاملاتِ هول انگیز را دیده بود
    Muntakhab, ii, 283
47. *Muntakhab*, ii, 283.
    Tabaqat, ii, 252.
    Akbarnama, iii, 308.
48. *Muntakhab*, ii, 282.

49. *Akbarnama*, iii, 308-9.
50. Ibid, 314.
51. *Muntakhab*, ii, 276-77.
52. Ibid, 277.
53. *Muntakhab*, ii, 279 هر کسی که مرید می‌گیرد با مجلسِ سماع یا نوعِ قلابی دارد
54. *Muntakhab*, ii, 291.
55. *Akbarnama*, iii, 335.
56. باشارتِ فتنه اندیشان آنجا [کابل] ببنگاله آمد و بشور افزایی و بدآموزی برنشست
    Akbarnama, iii, 292
57. *Akbarnama*, iii, 298, 309.
    Akbarnama, iii, 309 و به هرزه سرائی افروزینهٔ شورش شدی
58. *Tabaqat*, ii, 347.
59. *Muntakhab*, ii, 288.
    Tabaqat, ii, 355.
    Akbarnama, iii, 316.
60. *Akbarnama*, iii, 312-13.
61. Ibid, 316.
    Tabaqat, ii, 354.
    Muntakhab, ii, 287.
62. این بازیافت را چه توان نام نهاد؟ و طلب گاری بی هنگام را از کدامی گروه توان شمرد؟
    Akbarnama, iii, 316
63. *Akbarnama*, iii, 315-16.
64. Ibid, 319.
65. Ibid, 320.
66. Ibid, 333-34.
67. *Akbarnama*, iii, 337.
68. The well-paid forces are the least prone to defection. Akbar knew it well.
69. *Akbarnama*, iii, 337.
    Muntakhab, ii, 291.
70. *Akbarnama*, iii, 341.
71. Ibid, 327.
72. خلاصهٔ مضمون آنکه عرائض یکجهتی و نیک اندیشی پیهم می‌رسد و سرمایهٔ بالشِ توجه می‌گردد.
    Akbarnama, iii, 342 درین نزدیکی به نتایج آن اختصاص خواهد یافت
    Tabaqat, ii, 358.
    Muntakhab, ii, 292.
73. ملکِ ثانی
74. *Akarnama*,iii, 343 و بدکاران را تیزتر گرداند
    Tabaqat, ii, 358.
    Muntakhab, ii, 292.
75. او [ملکِ ثانی] از تصرف باز داشتند [مقید گردانیدند] - دران از خواجه بسا سخنان

جانبداری بظهور آمد - غبار شورش بلندی گرای شد- روزگـار نـاخن زنِ پرسـتار و آشـوبِ زمانه تازگی داشت

Akbarnama, iii, 343
Tabaqat, ii, 358.
Muntakhab, ii, 292.

76. *Akbarnama*, iii, 343 تا گوشمال کوته اندیشانِ دراز آز شود و تنبیه بدگوهرانِ کج گرا گردد
77. *Akbarnama*, iii, 343 از آنجا که روزگار از ناتوان بینانِ فرومایه بر آشفته بود و وقت نازک
Tabaqat, ii, 358-59.
Muntakhab, ii, 292-93.
78. *Tabaqat*, ii, 363.
Muntakhab, ii, 295.
79. Why did they break the seal of the letters instead of handing them over to the Khwaja? Perhaps, as the Malik would have said, because they also suspected the Khwaja of treasonable intentions. How could workers at a ferry have an inkling about the conspiracy which Akbar was trying to keep to himself alone!
80. *Akbarnama*, iii, 342-43.
Tabaqat, ii, 358-59.
Muntakhab, ii, 292-93.
81. Smith says that Nizam-ud-Din Ahmad declares only the second set of letters to be a forgery and it is Badauni who includes them all under the same category. *Akbar, The Great Mogul,* 196 (*Tabaqat*, ii, 363, *Muntakhab*, ii, 295.)
82. *Tabaqat*, ii, 363.
Muntakhab, ii, 295.
83. *Akbarnama*, iii, 342.
84. *Tabaqat*, ii, 358.
Muntakhab, ii, 292.
85. *Muntakhab*, ii, 275, 285.
Muntakhab, ii, 285 از جمله نا موافقان در مذهب و مشرب شمرده
Tabaqat, ii, 354.
Akbarnama, iii, 317.
86. *Muntakhab*, ii, 285.
87. *Tabaqat*, ii, 362.
Muntakhab, ii, 295.
Akbarnama, iii, 790.
88. *Akbarnama*, iii, 342. و ندانست که قلب کاری دو روزه ناپایـدار اسـت
اگر قدری نیایش درگاهِ ایزدی و لختی اخلاصِ خدیوِ عالم و برخی مهربانی بخلایق و انـدکی بی طمعی و کم آزاری باو بودی هر آئینه از قهر شهنشاهی بدین روز ننشستی
Akbarnama, iii, 343-44
89. و از کارشناسی بافته گویانِ عمامه بندِ شهر را از اختلاط باز می‌داشتند

Akbarnama, iii, 345.

90. *Akbarnama*, iii, 346-47.
91. *Akbarnama*, iii, 347,355.
92. Ibid, 347.
93. *Akbarnama*, iii, 355 و بعضی به هواخواهیِ آن غنوده بختِ نافرجام
94. *Akbarnama*, iii, 355.
95. و از نیروی ایزدی تأیید دستان زدهٔ این گروه نشدی - موئی سـفید و ریـشِ دراز نداشت و
خرقه زرق آلودِ کهن سالی روی ریا نمی‌افروخت
Ibid, 355.
96. *Akbarnama*, iii, 354.
97. Ibid, 357-58.
98. Ibid, 353.
99. *Akbarnama*, iii, 364, 356, 366.
100. Ibid, 356, 360, 365.
101. *Akbarnama*, iii, 367-69.
The Kingdom of Kabul was restored to Mirza Hakim, not to his sister as Smith says. (Smith, Akbar, *The Great Mogul*,200. *Akbarnama*, iii, 369. *Tabaqat*, ii, 362. *Muntakhab*, ii, 295.)
102. نسیم خوشدلی از فتح پور می‌آید   که پادشاهِ من ز راهِ دور می‌آید
چه دولت است قومش که مردم از دل خلق   هزار گونه طرب در ظهور می‌آید
خجسته باد بعالم قدوم او فیضی   که عالمی بمقام حضور می‌آید
Akbarnama, iii, 374
103. چنین مورثِ بزرگ که فرمان دهانِ وسعت آباد هند را بخاطر نرسیده بود به بهترین روش‌ها
بجائی آمد
Akbarnama, iii, 373.
104. *Muntakhab*, ii, 296.

The Anti-Climax

HIS NEW RELIGION

Chapter IV

Din-I-Ilahi

The rebellion in protest against Akbar's religious vagaries failed, because, in spite of them, Akbar had some sterling qualities. His rewards, his patronage, his sympathies, his whole treatment of his Muslim nobility, had not been disturbed by his ever changing religious views.

Besides, everyone could feel his sincerity. Many of his nobles loved him so much that they would not hold him responsible for his certain beliefs. They would give vent to their mortification by rebuking that 'infernal dog of a Birbar' and continue serving Akbar with unswerving loyalty.[1] At the same time, there were others who were attached to him by the 'milk-ties'[2] which were not less than blood-ties. They were in fact rather stronger, because there was no question of claiming the throne. They rested wholly on affection, sincere service and ample rewards. There were still others who were attached to Akbar inseparably, brought up by him from childhood. Such were the great Shahbaz, Abd-ur-Rahim Khan-Khanan, Aziz Khan Kuka, Zain Khan Kuka, Qutb-ud-Din Khan Atga, Sharif Khan Atga and many others.

Moreover, the whole strength of the Hindu nobility was ranged on Akbar's side: Raja Bhagwan Das, Kunwar Man Singh, Todar Mal, Rai Rai Singh and numerous others whom Akbar could safely trust.

But the rebellion chiefly failed, because the man to whom the traitors expected to lead the movement ruined the whole scheme. The only chance of success for Mirza Hakim was if Akbar's nobles were to change sides at the crucial moment. But they would not, unless he showed capabilities to lead them to success. He proved unequal to the task and the waverers became confirmed loyalists. A statesman conqueror like Akbar had not questioned the waverers and now accepted their loyalty at its face value.[3]

In spite of the fact that Akbar's religious beliefs had become publicly disturbing, nobles in Bihar and Bengal would not have thought of rebellion, if Mulla Tayyib and Purushottam Bakhshi in Bihar and Muzaffar Khan in Bengal had not been so tactless in their demands of arrears and so severe in 'branding the horses' of the nobles in these provinces. To make the situation utterly exasperating, the personnel of the Branding Department happened to be corrupt. Baba Khan Qaqshal would complain, "Seventy thousand rupees I have paid *'as presents'* so far, and not even one hundred horses have been passed and branded."[4]

What the nobles of Bihar and Bengal wanted was not a change in Akbar's religious beliefs, but the redemption or gradual payment of their arrears, mild and sympathetic policy in requiring them to accord to the new branding regulations along with the easy restoration of their jagirs, and the removal of their tyrannous immediate superiors. When once in revolt, they were afraid of the consequences. They had now to fight it out and work for final success. Political adventurers like Sharf-ud-Din Husain Mirza and others joined them for their own purposes.

And if Shah Mansur was heading a conspiracy in the court, he had a grudge against the royal favourite, Raja Todar Mal, the rival Diwan, who had once thrust him into prison[5] and, being malicious and revengeful,[6] could not be expected to hesitate in his destruction on the first opportunity.

Restiveness on religious grounds was not the primary cause of the rebellion. The rebels exploited it. They utilized it to the utmost.

Akbar did not think of abandoning his search after 'the Truth.' It never occurred to him that he was doing something wrong or injuring Muslim feelings. If some people were misconstruing his motives, they were the ignorant to be pitied or the mischievous to be severely dealt with. Just when the rebellion in the East was brewing and even after it had broken out, Akbar was discussing Christian doctrines with the Jesuits. Father Monserrate accompanied him in his Kabul expedition in the capacity of tutor of his second son, Prince Murad. On his way to Kabul, he visited Shaikh Jamal at Thanesar and after long talk about God between the Emperor and the saint, Akbar wanted him 'to relieve him of the bewilderment of his thoughts and the distress of his heart', and asked him why everyone was differing about God and 'the way to God'.[7] When the Emperor visited Tilla Bal Nath[8] near Rohtas in the North-Western Panjab, he met the 'jogis'[9] there and had a talk with them.[10]

On his return journey, at Lahore, Akbar appointed new sadrs, officers in charge of the bestowal, resumption, cut off and enquiry into the state endowment lands.

The Sadr Abd-ud-Nabi's jurisdiction comprised the whole empire. Akbar had also appointed some provincial sadrs. But the final organisation of the Sadarat with a provincial sadr in every province, in charge of the whole of the province, under the Chief Sadr at their head in the Central Government at the capital, had not as yet crystallised. Some of the sadrs now appointed were put in charge of more than one province, while others were entrusted with only a part of a province. The provinces of Delhi, Malwa and Gujarat were given in charge of Hakim Abu-l-Fath. Agra, Kalpi and Kalanjar were entrusted to Shaikh Faizi, the country from Hajipur to Saru to Hakim Humam, Bihar to Hakim Ali and Bengal to Hakim Ain-ul-Mulk.[11] For an immediate enquiry into the endowment lands in the Panjab, sadrs were appointed in its various 'doabs' (lands between every two rivers). They included Mulla Allahdad of Amroha, Mulla Allahdad of Sultanpur, Mulla Shah Muhammad of Shahpur and Mulla Sheri.[12]

These appointments reveal Akbar's changed policy towards the priestly class. If they were loyal, they might be endowed, taken into the Emperor's service, or appointed to government posts like Mulla Allahadad, Mulla Shah Muhammad and Mulla Sheri. They themselves might hold the most orthodox religious views, but they were not to denounce their Emperor in public, or engender sedition. At the same time we find that the important charges were not entrusted to the ecclesiastics but to men of letters and medicine, like Hakim (physician) Abu-l-Fath,

Hakim Humam, Hakim Ali, Hakim Ain-ul-Mulk and Shaikh Faizi, the poet laureate, who were the Emperor's most trusted courtiers and of liberal religious views. Akbar had become aware of the danger of concentration of power in the hands of the 'ulama', and was not prepared to revive it, once it had been broken.

In addition, men of similar type were appointed in the big cities to supervise the conduct of Qazis in the surrounding areas, to control this class having 'big turbans' (respectability) and 'long sleeves' (greed).[13]

Direct from his Kabul expedition, before reaching Fathpur, Akbar visited Mathura and went to see the Brahmans there.[14]

The saintly Aquaviva had been awaiting the Emperor's return, at the capital, to make the most glorious convert to the Catholic Church. On his return Akbar resumed religious discussions and invited Shaikh Qutb Jalesri to take part in them. The Shaikh said, 'Let a bonfire be lit and the Farangi and myself enter it. Whosoever comes out unhurt will be the follower of the Right Path.' The fire was lit, and the Shaikh, placing his hand round the waist of the Farangi, invited him, 'Han Bismillah! Yes, come on, in the name of God.' But the Farangi would not dare to.[15]

Akbar had already been concerned regarding the influence of the Shaikh in the neighbourhood of the capital.[16] This humiliation of his Jesuit friend and the resultant increase in the prestige of the Shaikh were decisive. He was exiled to Bhakkar. Some others also had to accompany him. Many others of the same type were exiled to various distant places, like Qandhar.[17]

To uproot the 'mashaikh'[18] from the places where they exercised public influence, sending them to distant places, was now the usual policy of Akbar. Shaikh Udhan's grandsons, the 'mashaikh' of Jaunpur—that origin of the ecclesiastical ruling against Akbar—were called to the court this year and along with their families were exiled to Ajmer, though an inadequate stipend was allowed to them. Similarly, Shaikh Husain, a scion of the Khwaja of Ajmer and in charge of his shrine, who had previously been exiled to Mecca, was now, after his return from there, sent to Bhakkar. He did not perform 'Taslim' and

'Kurnish' with scrupulous exactness this time as well, and it was taken to smack of disloyalty.[19] Bowing before a man—even if an emperor— is really a difficult task for a Muslim.

Genesis of the New Faith

Abu-l-Fazl and his Shia friends had rendered meritorious service to the cause of Islam! In the Shia doctrine the position of the Prophet is recognised as if imply to confirm the authority of the Imam. Otherwise the Imam is 'masum, innocent and infallible, and there are found one hundred and faults with the poor Prophet. And the condemnation of the first three Successors of the Prophet, in their every aspect of life, has been universal among the Shias of every type, because it was necessary to establish the hereditary right of succession against the democratic principle of election in whatever form it was there in the case of the first three Caliphs. These people would, therefore, enthusiastically discuss the traditions of 'Naqa-i-Qaswa', 'Attack upon the Quraish caravan', 'Question of the fourteen wives', 'Loss of the Prophet's tooth', 'Tahrim-i-Nisa', 'Problem of the Fidak gardens', 'Battle of Saffin' etc.[20], and condemn the Prophet, Abu Bakr, Umar and Usman—may God's peace be upon them—whom Muslims love more than their life, their wealth, their children, their all.

The result was that Akbar had been estranged from the Prophet and his Caliphs and from 'the modern religion'[21] of 'the destitute Arabs, all robbers and highwaymen.'[22] Moreover, they had been bringing out 'hidden meanings—far-fetched interpretation—of the Quranic texts and the 'Ahadis' of the Prophet. Hence Akbar would not believe in Prophethood, Revelation, the Quran as God's Word, its continuity, the Miracles, the Genesis, the Resurrection and Judgement, Immortality of the soul, angels and genii. Similarly, he had begun to consider Namaz (Islamic mode of worship), Roza (fasting a month a year), Haj (pilgrimage to Mecca) and the outward regulation of Islamic life as bereft of meaning.[23] Soon the 'Namaz ba jamaat' and the 'Azan' were abolished from the court. Islam was dubbed as mere 'taqlid', mimicing the people of the past.[24]

The Emperor did not care when a mosque was occupied by Hindus and turned into a sitting-room or when a Muslim monastery was occupied by Hindu guardsmen. And the graveyard within the city of Agra was levelled to the ground under his orders.[25]

If the Prophet of Islam was not safe from malignant criticism, others were not more sacred. Prophets like Davud (David) and others were also found fault with and traditions regarding them disbelieved in.[26]

When respect and love for the Prophet had decreased, names like Muhammad, Ahmad, Mustafa, originally the names and epithets of the Prophet, did not remain attractive for the Emperor. He preferred them to be exchanged for others.[27]

Neither did the Emperor consider it worthwhile to twist the throat to pronounce correctly letters particular to the language of 'the cursed eaters of lizards and imbibers of camel-milk (the Arabs)'. He was much pleased if they were pronounced otherwise.[28]

To learn the Arabic language and the study of 'fiqah', 'tafsir', 'hadis' etc. became a disqualification.[29]

One is surprised to learn of these developments under Muslim regime and many writers have rejected them and accused Badauni of false statement. But one who is aware of the Murjiite, Qadarite and Mutazilite thought, the Ismaili doctrines, and the Rational writings of the Buwayid period, can very well understand what was happening in the court and in the mind of the victim on the throne.

I have enumerated the rejections of 'the thinkers', Abu-l-Fazl and his friends. I may now turn to their suggestions. Shaikh Mubarak and the Shias to escape the domination of the 'ulama', like Abd-un-Nabi and Makhdum-ul-Mulk, and to feed the spiritual vanity of the Emperor, had been suggesting to him that he was 'the Imam of the Age'. Soon after they (not Shaikh Mubarak or Abu-l-Fazl) had begun to suggest something still higher.

The idea of the coming of a 'Promised Messiah' to renovate the world was a Jewish tradition which existed before the birth of Christ. The Jews rejected Christ as well as Muhammad as the 'Promised Messiah". Long after the Prophet of Islam, Muslims also began to await a Renovator. It was essentially a Shia doctrine. Imam Mahdi, the seventh or the twelfth Imam, was expected to re-appear and work for the spiritual regeneration and political glory of his followers. The whole of the world was said to fall under his sway and every nation to adopt his faith. Many Sunnis also began to believe in this appearance of a Renovator. Sometimes it was said to be the re-appearance of Christ, who was believed not to have been crucified but to have been 'lifted to heaven'. Judas Scariat the Traitor was said to have been miraculously metamorphosed into Christ's physical form and consequently crucified.

During the closing years of the sixteenth century A.D., as the first millennium of the Hijri era was coming to a close, it was believed to be the time for the appearance of the Renovator. The Shias like Sharif Amuli, Maulana Shirazi Jafardan and others suggested that the long awaited Renovator was the Emperor himself. Mahmud Basakhwani was said to have foretold that 'the Eraser of falsehoods' would make his appearance in the year 990 A. H. (1582 A.D.), as he would be the 'Sahib-i-Din-i-Haq (The Lord of the True Religion) and the numerical ('abjad') value of the words 'Sahib-i-Din-Haq' was 990. And Akbar was Sahib-i-Din-i-Haq. Other Shias even quoted Ali to the same effect. Some of them put forward in this connection quatrains, prophesying the advent of Imam Mahdi, attributed to Nasir Khusrau, the Ismaili 'dai'. One of them ran,

> In the year nine hundred and ninety (A.H.), I foresee one of the two things to happen. Either Mahdi or Dajjal[30] will appear.
>
> The former will renovate the Religion or the latter will devastate the land. I see the secrets that are still concealed.[31]

Akbar was declared to be 'the Lord of the Age', 'the Perfect Man', 'the Expected Mahdi', prostration before whom was permissible, reverence towards whom was a religious duty, and whose face was the 'Qibla-o-Kaba' to which one was to turn for one's wants and wishes.[32]

Hindus were not far behind their Muslim brethren in their suggestions. Brahmans composed Hindi verses as if by the sages of the past, foretelling the advent of a Great Emperor who would respect the Brahman and protect the cow, and having written them on old scraps of paper showed them to the Emperor, who was much pleased.[33] Such prophecies made in the past seem to be very palatable to the Emperor.[34] Whether they were real or spurious mattered little. Akbar had determined to translate them into reality.

The power of the priestly class had been broken. The influence of the saintly classes put an end to. The nightmare of a political rebellion on religious grounds had appeared and disappeared. Akbar now felt at liberty to indulge in his religious freaks.[35] He could not do it earlier, because he was afraid of the blind followers of the past.[36] The suppression of the rebellion in the East and the North-West had established the triumph of Reason[37] (Akbar's vagaries), and the Victorious Reason was now prepared to promulgate its own Religion.

The condemnation of Islam, the Prophet of Islam, and his successors at the hands of free-lance scholars was merely destructive. It had no constructive aspect. They demolished a superstructure with its dark corners as well as its charming balconies and airy avenues, and had nothing to replace it. And whatever debris remained was not attractive enough for Akbar. They made him disgusted with the old Islam. They prepared him to become the New Prophet, the Mahdi. He got ready for this. But he would not follow the lines they indicated. So far he had been following them. Now it was their turn to follow him and accept, at least in words, his every whim and answer an abject 'Yes, Sire'.

Islam had become something common with Akbar. He had known it for long. Muslim experts themselves had shown him that it was not all good. He had become satiated with it.[38] Change for him was the spice of life. He turned to taste and relish what other chefs had prepared.[39] Of the Christian, the Hindu, the Jain, the Zoroastrian religions, the last named had appealed most to his imagination, because it was associated with the Grand Spectacle of the Chosroes of Iran. He was fascinated by the ancient Royal Festivals of Persia and the huge red flames of the Perpetual Light of Yazdan, ever leaping up in the Fire Temple within the Royal Palace at Madain. He had ordered a similar fire to be kept burning in his own palace and Abu-l-Fazl had been made its High Priest.[40]

It was on the Zoroastrian Sacred Day, Nauroz, in 1582, that the Iranian Festivals were introduced[41] and 'the wheel of Akbar Shah came into motion'.

One thousand years since the ministry of Muhammad had passed. The age of his religion was said to be over.[42] To declare this, coins were struck bearing the date, 1000 A.H.[43]

A new age had begun. One definite period had come to an end.[44] A compact history of this period of a thousand years was ordered to be written.[45]

The Hijri era referred to a man of the past. A great man had again appeared. To perpetuate his name[46] the Ilahi era was inaugurated, commencing from the first Nauroz after Akbar's accession to the throne. The months of the year were given old Iranian names and Zoroastrian Ids or festivals, fourteen in number, were introduced.[47]

The celebrations of the Festival of Nauroz were the most spectacular. The festivities went on for weeks together. The Mina Bazar was held.[48] Ranks and honours and promotions were bestowed upon the officials and the Rajas. 'Peshkashs'[49] from the 'umara', the Provincial governors and the Rajas were received. Many of them presented themselves in the court to pay their homage afresh. The spoils of war: gold, silver, pearls, jewels, rubies, diamonds, swords, daggers, hawks, slaves, horses, elephants, were all presented to the Emperor by the 'vakils'[50] of the generals fighting on various fronts. And it was at the Nauroz Festival every year that the Commandments of the Royal Prophet were issued henceforth.

Akbar was 'the Chosen of God', 'the Prophet of God',[51] 'the Representative of God',[52] 'the Expression of God',[53] and hence 'sajdah' or prostration was considered due to him. It was made the mode of paying respects to the Emperor.[54]

In this instance I was inclined to accuse Badauni of unwarranted exaggeration. I thought he was referring to some mode of paying respect in which one had to bow a bit. But, at least once in life, frankly and candidly Abu-l-Fazl records a fact: actual 'sajdah' was paid to the Emperor.[55]

The 'umara' had to pay it as a necessary evil. But Abu-l-Fazl explains it like this: 'They actually prostrate before Akbar, but they avow that they really prostrate before God.'[56] There were precedents for this. The Zorostrians would worship fire and explain that they were really worshipping Yazdan. Jains would worship the idol of Mahavir and explain that they were really worshipping the Creator. Hindus would worship one thousand and one stone statues and clay models and explain that they were really worshipping the Supreme Being. Christians would worship the images of the Virgin and Christ or the Crucifixion and explain that they were really worshipping God. What was the harm, if instead of these dead symbols, the living one of the all ruling Emperor was substituted on the pedestal of the Royal Throne in the Temple of the Mughul Court?

And the phrase 'Allah-o-Akbar', 'God is Great', was given the highest prominence.[57] Two years later it was ordered to be written at the top of every Royal Farman and on all sorts of letters and communications, official or otherwise.[58] We find it on the title pages of books written after this date by the court writers.

No one has explained so far why this phrase was given so much importance and currency. No contemporary of Akbar cared to point out its significance. The matter is further confused, because Akbar had liked it for the legend on his Royal seal and coins a few years before, in 1577.

A hypothesis may be offered. Akbar had begun to think himself 'the Prophet of the Age', but he had not dared to express it. Neither was it ever done in spoken words or on paper. Sometime back, in 1579, his favourites had begun to repeat within the palace the words: 'There is no god but God, and Akbar is the Caliph of God.' The word 'Caliph of God' was adopted which was in use for Muslim rulers. Still it resembled too much the Muslim confession of Faith, which reads: 'There is no god but God, and Muhammad is the Prophet of God', and had contributed towards the Insurrection of 1579-81. Akbar wanted no repetition. Hence we do not hear of it, when the New Religion was formally enunciated on the New Year Day in March, 1582.

But Akbar's religion must have a Confession of Faith and Declaration of his Ministry. I think it was found in the words 'Allah-o-Akbar'. Some years before, when Akbar wanted it to be the legend of his seal and coins, he liked it, as he himself pointed out, because the word 'akbar' was therein.[59] This time the phrase had acquired a new significance. It was not being taken as 'God is Akbar (Great)' or 'Akbar (the Emperor) is God', but as 'God—Akbar (the Emperor)'. 'God and Akbar'—that was the confession and Declaration. Besides God and Akbar, none was of any account. It was tantamount to saying: 'There is no god but God, and Akbar is the Prophet of God.' And the phrase had the advantage of declaring this status of Akbar in no words, and has also the simple meaning of 'God is Great'.

The preceding hypothesis is suggested by the fact that it had already become the usual practice of the court writers not to pay customary respects[60] to the Prophet of Islam after the Praise of God and before the panegyric of the ruling prince in introducing their books. The writers, after the Praise of God, went directly to the Royal eulogy. The respects due to the Prophet were omitted.[61] Books of writers like Faizi still exist with this qualification, supporting to-day what Badauni wrote more than three hundred years ago.

The Emperor called this new trend in beliefs and practices as 'Tauhid-i-Ilahi' or the Monctheism.[62]

Besides the cavalry organised under the 'umara' commanding various number of soldiers, the Mughul Emperors had an army of retainers directly under them. These gentleman troopers served the Emperors in individual capacity. None of them had any one else under him. They were called 'yakas' *i.e.* singles. The Emperor gave them the name of 'Ahadis' *i.e.* monotheists.[63]

At the festival of Nauroz in 1582, Akbar declared thousands of his slave-soldiers to be free and named them as 'chellas' *i.e.* disciples, in the term of 'jogis'.[64]

Personal slaves and personal retainers were to form the mucleus of the following of the New Prophet!

Thus was enunciated among the festivities of the Nauroz Din-i-Ilahi Akbar Shahi.

And this is how a candidate was initiated into the Order. The man would take off his turban from his head and keeping it on the palm of his hand would place his head on the sacred feet of the Holy Emperor. After some time 'the Lord of the Form and Meaning' would raise him up and place his turban on his head.[65]

This ritual is explained thus by Abu-l-Fazl, the Vice-regent of the New Prophet. The initiate had taken off his turban from his head to declare that, by virtue of his good fortune and auspicious stars, he had shed egoistic self-adoration and self-importance from his head, and, by placing his head upon the feet of the Royal Saint, he had pronounced that he was offering the sacrifice of his head in search of the Real Life. By raising him up the Jagat Guru had as if declared. 'Brave man, raise up yourself with my support and from the existence-like non-existence come into the Real existence.'[66]

Then the novice was given the 'Shist', on which was written 'the Great Name (of God) and the Divine Magic (or the Heavenly Mystery): Allah-o-Akbar',[67] and he was instructed that " 'the Holy Shist' and 'the Holy Glance (of the Royal Prophet)' would not err (in guiding him)."[68]

After their initiation whenever the disciples met each other, one was to shout, 'Allah-o-Akbar', 'God is Great', and the other in response, 'Jall-i-Jalal-Hu', 'Great is His Jalal (Glory)'.[69] Whether the word 'Jalal', meaning glory, was being taken as His or God's glory or it was for Akbar himself, whose another name was Jalal (Jalal-ud-Din), is not certain. In fact ambiguous phrases were being used and the 'Secrets' being created.

The question of the 'Shist' has also remainded an enigma. Abu-l-Fazl says that a 'Shist' was given, but does not explain what it was. Badauni, on the other hand, tells us that a small portrait of the Emperor was given to the disciples at the time of initiation[70] and nowhere mentions any 'Shist'. The result is that Smith has been led to the conclusion that a 'Shist' as well as a small portrait of the emperor was given to the disciples and is at a loss to explain the former.[71]

Actually the 'Shist' and the portrait were one and the same thing. It was the same small portrait of the Emperor on which were written the words 'Allah-o-Akbar'. This conclusion may be drawn from the fact that Badauni mentions a small portrait and Abu-l-Fazl a 'Shist' given at the time of initiation. Moreover, there is a significant adjective in the text of *Ain.* When Abu-l-Fazl writes about the 'Shist', he says that a 'Personal (the Emperor's) Shist' was given.[72] If we read this with Badauni, the explanation is clear.

Abu-l-Fazl conveys the impression that the Name of God on the Shist would guide the initiate. Now if it turns out to be a portrait of the Emperor, how would it guide the disciple? The answer is not far to seek, if we remember the Ibadatkhana discussions. The idols of men-like gods, such as Rama and Krishna, were explained to be the symbols of God. The images of the Holy Virgin and Christ also formed the images of the two of the Trinity. All of them had been said to lead men towards God. And according to most of the 'Sufis', disciples are first to imagine of their Murshid (the Guiding saint) before they began to imagine of God. From concentration on an image in mind to concentration on an image on paper, was not a very long step.

The Holy Image of the Emperor, the emblem of sincerity and an introduction to guidance and felicity, was placed in a silken casement, studded with pearls and jewels, and kept within their turbans by the Royal disciples.[73]

The talk about the real-existence and the existence like non-existence might have been, to some extent, the contribution of the Jesuits. According to the Christian doctrine, man acquires life only when he is baptised.

There were four grades of sincerity for Akbar's disciples, foregoing (i) one's wealth, (ii) wealth and life, (iii) wealth, life and honour, and (iv) wealth, life, honour and religion.[74] It shows that there could be disciples retaining something of their own religion. It was only in the final stage that they discarded their previous religion, explained as 'nothing but mimicing the people of the past',[75] and adopted the Religion of 'the Lord of Mysteries, knowing the Real meanings behind the words.' The disciples were thus to approach closest to their lord by stages.

Some of the most anxious to secure Royal favours would sign a document saying, 'Myself, so and so, son of so and so, of my own accord and with love of heart, abandon the outward Islam which I inherited from my father and forefathers, and enter into Din-i-Ilahi of Akbarshah, adopting all the four grades of sincerity, sacrificing my wealth, my life, my honour and my religion.' And these 'writs to damnation' were handed over to Abu-l-Fazl, the High Priest of the New Religion.[76]

The Sun-worship

Akbar named his religion as 'the Monotheism', but actually he accepted a Divine Rival. Fire seems to have been worshipped by him as an inanimate symbol of God. But to the Sun were certainly attributed superlative traits of a Living God.[77] The favourite writers in the court whenever naming Sun in their writings would add 'Great is His Glory', as was the custom in the case of God Himself.[78]

The Zoroastrian and Hindu influences had merged in this respect. During the Nauroz Festival the emperor would openly worship and prostrate before Fire–the Sign out of the Signs of God, the Light out of the Lights of God.[79]

When one of the most favourite and sincerest disciples died, a fire-amber was said to have been placed upon his tongue at the time of burial.[80]

The Sun was acknowledged as the Expression of God, the Ripener of cereals and fruit, the Grower of trees and verge, the Light-giver and the Life-giver of the world.[81] It was due to his entry into Aries in March (coming into the new life of Spring after the death of Winter) that the Day of Nauroz was sanctified[82] and made the occasion of spectacular festivities rivalling those of ancient Egypt, Persia, Greece and Rome in honour of the Sun-god. The Emperor publicly worshipped and prostrated before the Sun during these festivities.[83]

Akbar used to worship the Sun every day also in the morning, in the evening, at midday and at midnight. At midday worship he would repeat in Hindi one thousand and one names and epithets of the Golden God, would catch hold of both of his ears, administer blows on his ear lobes and go through many other similar acts.[84] —all mysteries known to him and the 'wily pandits'.

At midnight and daybreak drums were beaten in honour of the advent of the Resplendent Emperor of the Heavens.[85]

No animal was allowed to be slaughtered on Sunday—the Day of the Sun.[86] When the people would bring cups of water to the Emperor, so that he might blow on the water to give it healing qualities, he would hold it up to the Sun as well.[87]

The day break and the Sun God appears in the East. The East was to be honoured therefore. Akbar began to sleep with his head towards the East and feet towards the West—the Kaba side![88] Similarly, the Royal disciples, on their death, were to be buried with their head towards the East and feet towards the West.[89] When one of the closest disciples died, at the time of burial there was left an opening in his grave towards the East, so that the 'sin-wiping' light of the Sun might fall on his face every morning.[90]

Until a writ from the authorities of the State Treasury regarding the loans from the State was acquired, a dead man was not allowed to be buried. Meanwhile, his body was ordered to be kept in the graveyard on the Eastern side of the city. This was also done in honour of the Sun, the Lord of the East.[91]

Birbar was killed in the Afghan hills in 1586, when the Mughul army was retreating. Akbar was sorry that he could not be 'purified in fire' at his death. Then he consoled himself, saying, "He did not need this purification; the heat of the Great Resplendent was sufficient to do this for him."[92]

The Zoroastrian influence is evident in connection with some funeral rites as well. The Hindu disciples, male as well as female, called Darshanyas, were ordered to drown their dead in the river, with a quantity of cereal and a brick bound round their necks. If there was no river nearby, they were to be burnt or hung from a tree[93]—certainly to be eaten away by birds like vultures as was and is the custom of Parsis.

Regarding the respect shown to fire and light the Zoroastrian influence reached niceties. When the lights were lit in the court at dusk, the courtiers were to stand up in honour of the little flames[94] which had appeared to officiate for the Lord of the Light.

Akbar became fond of everything related to the Chosroes. He seems to have liked their names also. He named the first-born of his eldest son as Khusrau (Chosroe) and that of his second son as Rustam. To his three other grandsons he gave the names of Parvez, Tahmuras and Hoshang.[95]

If one is born a Hindu, he remain a Hindu, whichever god he may worship. Thus thousands of Hindus at the capital became Akbar's disciples. The 'crafty Brahmans' would explain that Akbar was also an 'Avatar'(incarnation) of the Supreme Being, like Rama, Krishna and the rest, and stringed together one thousand and one names of the Akbar-Avatar for repetition. These disciples would gather in hundreds under the Audience Balcony (Jharoka) every morning to have a glimpse of the Divine Face. They would not take or drink anything or begin their day's work, unless they had a look ('darshan') on their God-in-the-Form-of-Akbar.[96] That is why they became known as 'Darshanyas' or 'the People of the Glimpse.'

Every morning they would repeat one thousand and one names of the Akbar-Avatar and await outside, while the Emperor would worship Surya Dev and repeat his one thousand and one names within the palace. When the Emperor had finished his devotions, he would appear on the Balcony. As soon as he came into the sight of the Darshanyas, they fell upon their knees.[97] Thousands of men in abject prostration before Akbar! No one in modern history enjoyed greater deification.

Beliefs and Commandments of the Royal Prophet

Akbar had begun to believe in the doctrine of Transmigration of souls and considered it impossible for the soul to exist without a body.[98]

He also believed, as 'the all-knowing Brahmans' explained to him, that the soul of a perfect man departed through the crown of his head, the tenth opening of the body, with a thundering noise, which was a proof of his salvation and the sign of his soul entering into the body of some magnificent emperor. That is why Akbar had the crown of his head shaved and let his hair grow at the sides.[99]

The Transmigration of souls was an important doctrine of Akbar's cult, explaining life after death and reward and punishment for one's deeds hereafter, which was adopted from Hinduism.

Due to the influence of association with Hindus Akbar had discarded taking onion, garlic and beef the last named being abhorrent to the Hindus.[100] The cow was sacred to them, because it was, as the Brahmans would explain in public, so useful for agriculture and dairy products, providing subsistense for human life.

Akbar prohibited beef for his disciples, not for Muslims in general, as he is usually accused of. After some time he extended the injunction prohibiting also the meat of the buffalo, sheep, horse and camel.[101]

The meat of an animal was said to convey its characteristics. The Emperor said, 'The meat of the tiger and the wild boar should have been permissible, so that their courage might be transmitted to man.'[102] Akbar was not adding meat dishes, so repulsive to Muslims, as this remark has generally been interpreted, but merely giving an opinion.

The Emperor had rather begun to dislike meat and refrained from it for many days a month. He considered this abstention from physical pleasure as a mortification of his ego, yielding spiritual elevation.[103]

Soon this abstention was extended to more than six months a year and the Emperor intended to forego this pleasure entirely. The days of abstention included Sundays, the Sun's Days (Badauni clearly brings out Sunday as the Day of the Sun), the day of Nauroz and the following seventeen days, the first day of every solar month, the days of eclipse, the days of monthly festivals, the whole of the month in which the Emperor was born, extending into the next, making the whole span of as many days as years of life completed by the Emperor.[104]

The Royal disciples were also admonished to try their utmost to abstain from meat. They were ordered not to take meat throughout the month of their birth and not to eat what they had themselves hunted.[105]

Animal slaughter was prohibited throughout the empire, under severe punishments, on many of the days when the Emperor did not take meat, including the extraordinarily long period connected with the birth of the Emperor.[106] Muslims, of course, must have smarted under this prolonged restriction.

Some writers, like Vincent Smith, have explained Akbar's abstention from meat and prohibition of animal slaughter on various days as due to Jain influence,[107] as the Jains are the exponents of the sacredness of life in any form. Their saints would keep their mouths covered with cloth, so that even a tiny moth might not be destroyed by entering into their mouths. Abu-l-Fazl also says that it was due to the compassionate heart of the Emperor. But Badauni clearly says that Akbar did it as an ascetic practice, in respect of Hindu sentiments, in honour of the Sun and various astronomical positions, and in sanctification of his own birth.[108] Only this much Jain influence might be conceded that Akbar honoured the Sun-god by stopping slaughter in his name, instead of offering him bloody sacrifices. Akbar would not eat animal flesh. But slaughtering thousands of animals in the Qamargha hunts and killing thousands of men in wars remained a fair game for him. How would Smith explain this phenomena? It is a poor apology to put forward political reasons or talk of the dual personality of Akbar.

From Akbar's diet I come to his mode of apparel and other practices in which Hindu influence is manifest.

Akbar had begun to shave his beard and liked it thus. All of his favourite courtiers followed him in this respect, and it had become the symbol of love and devotion to the Emperor.[109]

On the death of a disciple's parent, he was to shave his moustaches, head and eyebrows, as Akbar himself did when his mother and when his foster-mother died.[110]

The silk dress and gold jewellery Islam reserved for the fair sex. The man's share was the sword and the soldier's life. But Akbar, like Hindu Rajas, gave vogue to these adornments for men. Even the Muftis[111] of the new regime luxuriated in them.[112]

Akbar began to have also a 'qashqa', 'tilak' or the sacred Hindu mark, on his forehead.[113] What mysterious efficacy of this red or yellow smudge on the forehead was explained to him is not known.

The Prophet of Islam prohibited the making of images of man or animals of any kind, as they had all been worshipped at one time or another; the Egyptian religion had been full of animal-worship—of Bulls and Rams, Dog-headed Baboons and Cats, Cobra-hoods and Vulture-heads—and because there was still chance for human thought to relapse into ancient paganism.[114] But Akbar encouraged painting and portraiture, arguing that it led to the glorification of God, and the realisation of the helplessness of man: he could draw and paint but he could not make his pictures come alive.[115]

The Emperor now also liked Hindu names, such as Bishvatan which he gave to the grandson of Abu-l-Fazl, his spiritual vicegerent.[116]

The Hindu Festival of Rakhi was celebrated in the court. The Brahmans would come and tie the sacred string round the wrist of the Emperor.[117] Similarly, the Hindu Festivals of Dasahra and Divali were celebrated with great rejoicing.[118]

On the occasion of the Shivrat—the Night of Shiva—the Emperor would attend the assemblies of the 'jogis'. He would listen to their mystic talk and eat and drink with them.[119]

Akbar instructed his disciples to give a feast, for the spiritual peace of their soul after death, in their lifetime, on the day of their every birthday.[120]

Usury was put an end to by the Prophet of Islam. It had made a section of society useless to the community. They would get money without work—unproductive hands. Jews were the worst exponents of this institution. But Akbar, like the Hindus, legalised it and his Imperial Treasury charged interest on loans proffered to various nobles. It became a source of state income.[121]

A very regrettable addition to the judicial administration was the result of Hindu and perhaps also of Christian influence. Akbar introduced trial by ordeal. The accused was to hold a red-hot bar of iron in his hand or to dip his hand in boiling oil. If his hand was burnt, he was 'proven guilty'. Another method for the accused to prove his innocence was to dive in water and keep under the surface till an arrow flung from a bow was carried back by someone.[122] Akbar's belief in supernatural intervention here betrayed him, for one wonders to find an administrator like Akbar replacing justice by chance or condemnation without trial. How far this method was actually put into practice by the newly appointed Brahman judges for the Hindus is not known. Certainly the Muslim personnel of the Judicial administration—Qazis throughout the Empire—never adopted it. Neither was it meant for them. The Islamic law does not recognise this barbarity.

The dog, the wild boar, and the pig were unclean to the Prophet of Islam and hence for Muslims. Akbar liked them—the dog, because of its fidelity, but the wild boar, because the Brahmans explained to him that once God Almighty had descended on the earth in the form of a wild boar.[123] The Emperor was, for some time at least, in the habit of taking a look early in the morning at a wild boar—once the Form of God Himself.[124]

The inhuman doctrine of untouchability also did not fail to touch the Emperor. Akbar, according to Abu-l-Fazl, ordered his disciples not to dine with butchers, fishermen or bird-catchers. Badauni goes to the extent of saying that whosoever would dine with a butcher was to lose his hand as punishment and one who dined with a butcher's relatives was to lose his first finger.[125]

The Emperor prohibited people in the lower strata of society from acquiring knowledge. Orders to this effect were issued to the government officials in cities, because knowledge made them mischievous![126] And the Prophet of Islam had ordered every Muslim, man and woman, to acquire knowledge and go to seek it even in distant land. There were no spiritual strata of society. There was to be no monopoly by the priest. No one was to hold the Keys of Heaven. There was none between God and man. The Word of God was for every one, for the sovereign and the sweeper alike.

So much we may attribute to Hindu and Zoroastrian influence. But Akbar's imagination was still thirsty for unknown wonders, still in search of something strange and foreign and romantic. At least a little more was supplied from overseas.

Three missions of Jesuits from Portuguese Goa were

received at the court and their endless efforts were not without fruit. Akbar adopted the Kernel of Christianity: the worship of the Images of the Holy Trinity. A Royal Chapel of canvas was set up. The Image were placed on the altar. The gongs would toll and Akbar would kneel before the Holy Images,[127] with fervour no less than that of an Ignatius Loyola.

Now I turn to those regulations of Akbar's cult which touched life more intimately. A man was not to marry his first cousin, not on any scientific ground, but because such a close relationship—due to familiarity perhaps—did not excite the highest passion[128] which was considered so necesssary in conceiving healthy children. Here Hindu influence can be discerned. They do not marry even a distant cousin, nor even any one belonging to the sub-castes of father and mother and a few other near relatives.

A widow or an unmarried woman, who had reached the menopause, was not to marry.[129]

If the wife was twelve years senior to him, the husband was not to mate with her.[130]

A man was not to cohabit with a pregnant, old or barren woman, or with very young girls[131] (unable to produce children easily).

A boy was not to be circumcised till he was twelve years of age and even at that time he was free to have it or reject it.[132] The Hindus must have emphasized its uselessness, because they themselves did not do it.

One of the most unfortunate events in human history has been that Christ had not married before his crucifixion. Consequently, the early Christian Saints and Fathers, who actually formulated Christianity, as a reaction against the licence of the existing religions, made celibacy the highest ideal of human life. The woman was declared to be 'the temptress', 'the tool of Satan'. Muhammad raised woman to her rightful place. She was declared 'the Queen of man's heart and home', 'the fragrance of life'. She was given the right of acceptance or rejection of her would-be husband at the time of marriage, the right of inheritance and the privilege of securing separation, if she did not want to live with her husband any longer.

Muhammad's ministry was the greatest revolution in human thought since Christ declared the Kingdom of God, in which there were no slaves and no Estates. The Caesars saw their mighty empire crumbling to pieces before the force of the new thought and tried as if they could smother his immortal Word by railing him on the Cross and degrading him by gibbeting beside thieves. Glorified is the memory of even those two thieves. Muhammad raised woman to her rightful place, but one of the aspects of his great revolution was that he completely secularized sex.

Akbar was again sanctifying it. Muhammad asked a husband and wife to take bath in the morning after their night together—for the sake of cleanliness. Akbar abolished this and argued, 'How is it that the discharge of such a pure thing as semen that has been the cause of the birth of so many saints and pious men, should make us unclean? It behoves rather bathing and purifying oneself before coitus.'[133] Whence came this idea? Perhaps from Hinduism where Puranic literature is full of instructions to anoint oneself with butter before coitus and where 'Shivlingam', the stone Phelic of Shiva, is anointed with Holy Water and garlanded with flowers in temples day and night.

Sex was being sanctified, because of procreation as is clear from the argument proffered in support of bathing before coitus and from the instructions regarding sex life enumerated above. Otherwise individual love was not being recognised.

Hinduism was not a missionary religion. One was a Hindu because one was born a Hindu. A Hindu was not allowed to marry a non-Hindu. If a Hindu and a Muslim of opposite sex fell in love, the obvious way out, therefore, was that the former would become Muslim and they would marry. Akbar prohibited such marriages. The lovers were not let together. They were forcibly separated by the agents of law.[134]

The Regulation prohibiting such marriages and most of the Regulations which follow were not for Akbar's disciples only; they were for general application.

A man was not to have more than one wife, except where the first one proved barren.[135]

Akbar prohibited the marriage of girls under fourteen and boys under sixteen. He also prohibited marriages between the young and the old. This Rgulation was enforced by law. Tavi Begis or the Supervisors of Marriages were appointed. No couple could marry unless they had appeared in person before the authorities, had been examined personally by them, and a certificate of age had been issued for marriage.[136]

Hindu widows were allowed to remarry, if they liked. No one was to force them otherwise.[137]

Hindu widows were not to be compelled to undergo 'sati'.[138]

Hindu girls, who had been married in childhood and whose husbands died before the consummation of marriage, were prohibited from undergoing 'sati'.[139]

Akbar encouraged the study of literary and scientific subjects, like astronomy, mathematics, medicine, philosophy, history, poetry and romance,[140] as against theology.

The parents, who sold their children as slaves under straitened circumstances, were given the right of bring them back, whenever they could afford to.[141]

A certain portion of legal cases between Hindus were to be decided by wise Brahmans instead of Qazis.[142]

If a Hindu had been converted to Islam in childhood or by force, he was permitted to re-convert to his previous religion, if he liked.[143]

The building of churches, fire-temples and idol-temples was permitted.[144]

Conversion from one religion to another was universally allowed.[145]

Games of chance had been prohibited by Islam and it was one of the duties of 'Muhtasibs', officials of 'Hisba' (a section of the police), to check gambling; Akbar legalised it, and a Gambling Apartment was set up in the court. The courtiers could borrow money for the purpose from the Royal Treasury, on the spot—on interest, no doubt—if they were or became short of money.[146]

Prostitution has existed in every age and in every country. Muslim countries were not an exception, though Islam had prohibited it and made it a state crime. The state had to suffer it, the nature of man being what it is. But Akbar dropped it from the list of crimes against the state. Whosoever liked could go to a prostitute after giving his name and address to the state official in charge of the prostitution quarter. Every one was allowed to bring a prostitute to his house for the night on the same condition.[147]

The flirts and the shrews were told to go to this quarter of the city and conduct this business.[148]

For the courtiers there was one restriction. If any one of them wanted to have a girl who had not cohabited with anyone so far, he had to apply for permission to the Emperor, through the official in charge of the quarter, otherwise they were severely reprimanded and sent to prison. One of those who were detected in this default was the Royal Prophet's own Deputy High Priest, Raja Birbar, who had taken all the four oaths of fidelity to obey his Guru. He was away from the court when the secret came out. When he learnt of the disclosure, he made up his mind to become a recluse and disappear,[149] true to the traditions of the Great gods of his Hindu religion. When Indra Dev, the Lord of Rain and Thunderbolts, had ravished the wife of another god, he metamorphosed himself into a winged insect and disappeared into the petals of a lotus, standing in the Lake Manasarowar.

Intoxicants were prohibited by Islam. In spite of it liquor continued in all Muslim countries to be the luxury of the princes and the rich and those who liked and could afford it. This crime against the state was usually connived at. Still the religious prohibition was a mental hindrance to full enjoyment. Daqiqi, the well known poet of Persia, fervently desires the 'Mazhab-i-Zardhashti', the Religion of Zoroaster, when he pines for wine, because it was not prohibited in that religion. In Akbar's cult liquor was allowed, though drunkenness was prohibited and was severely dealt with.[150] Even the Qazis and Muftis of the new regime, like Mir Sadr-jahan, Mufti of the Empire, and Mir Abd-ul-Hayy, Mir-i-Adl or Qazi, would ask for goblets—not empty—to please the Emperor, and he, the 'Lord of the world', sipping the 'wisdom-increasing wine', would repeat the verse:

In the reign of the Padshah, who connives at
shortcomings and forgives crimes,
Muftis are drinking from cups and Qazis have
lifted decanters to their lips.[151]

The Abolition of Jizya

Another outcome of Akbar' policy was the abolition of Jizia. The poll tax called Jizia was in vogue in the Persian Empire of Chosroes before the advent of Islam, and the soldiers were exempted from its payment.

When Muslim power expanded, this tax was levied upon their non-Muslim subjects, offering in return security of life and property, toleration of their religions and houses of worship, churches, synagogues etc., and exemption from military service. The women, the children and the old were not taxed as they were incapable of military service. Only the adult had to pay this tax at the rate of 12 dirhams or Rs. 3.12 once a year for the lower classes, 24, dirhams for the middle and 48 dirhams for the rich, holding property worth more than 10,000 dirhams, payable in one, two or four instalments. It was not a crushing burden, as some writers have maintained. A tax instead of military service was not unknown in Europe. Edward I of England collected Shield Money. Islam for the first time in history presented to the world religious toleration at this simple charge,[152] and this mostly due to the military cost, because the Muslims at that time well appreciated the value of nationalized military power. Napoleon failed, when his forces failed in this qualification. The British power in India was based upon the absence of national and political consciousness. As soon as it had developed, Indians were to be found struggling against the British. Non-Muslims began to rise against the Mughuls, when their Muslim forces weakned.

The payment of Jizia in return for the security of life and freedom in religion was not taken as persecution by the Christians or others at the time of the Muslim conquest, but as the most welcome alternative to religious persecution. I may quote one illustration. The invincible Khalid was fighting on the Western front against the Byzantine power in Syria. The city of Hims (Emesa) had been occupied. Due to some strategic reason, he decided to leave the city. He called in the Bishop of Hims and returned to him the proceeds of the Jizya collected from the Christians, explaining that as Muslims were not in a position to guarantee the promised security throughout the year, the tax collected had to be returned to the tax-payers. The Muslims left and the Christians closed the gates of the city. Bidding farewell to the Muslims, the Bishop added, 'We shall pray in our Churches for your return. May we open the gates of our city upon you again and not upon the Byzantines', because Christians in Syria were being persecuted by the Byzantine Christians on sectarian grounds. Similar was the woeful tale of the Christians of Egypt. The Jizia collecting Muslims were not the religious persecutors but the liberators of the persecuted on religious grounds.

And if non-Muslims would render military help, they were not to pay the Jizia. Certain Christians, during the Muslim military operations in Syria and Palestine, rendered valuable help to the Muslims. It was taken as active military service by the Caliph Umar the Just, and they were exempted from the payment of Jizia. Later on all non-Muslim government servants were exempted from this payment.

Hence, when Rajputs and other Hindus were rendering valuable military and civil services to Akbar and he abolished Jizia, it was not something revolutionary.

Moreover, when the Muslims conquered and occupied Persia, Syria, Egypt and other countries, agricultural classes were not ejected from the lands they were holding. By law the land belonged to the conquering people. Umar acknowledged their rights, but his wisdom saved millions from destruction, Muslims were not allowed to eject the previous holders and possess the land. The revenue from these lands was instead made the communal property. Each would receive a stipend from this income. The non-Muslims were given the right of permanent occupation of the land in return for the payment of the land revenue called Khiraj.[153] The Khiraj-paying subjects did not pay Jizia, because Khiraj was as if inclusive of Jizia. The Jizia was paid mostly by the ubran population.

Akbar collected land revenue at the rate of one third of the produce, which was the rate of Khiraj, with the utmost care not to miss a penny, and Khiraj was inclusive of the Jizia. Hence, when Akbar abolished Jizia, it was abolished in the case of the fractional urban population of Hindus only.

But Akbar abolished Jizia neither because he had no legal right to collect it from the Hindus as they were serving him on the battle-field, nor because the land revenue he collected was inclusive of it. It seems to me that the abolition of Jizia by Akbar has not been interpreted in its true perspective so far. Abu-l-Fazl writes that the Jizia was abolished in the beginning of the year 1564,[154] and every historian has accepted this statement at its face value, without comparing it with the information in other sources or in the same source so tactfully camouflaged.

The first reason Abu-l-Fazl gives for the abolitions of Jizia in 1564 is as follows: 'The Jizia was collected from the non-Muslims in the past, because Muslims and non-Muslims were enemies of each other. Now when the non-Muslims are serving the State and have positive faith in the Emperor and following their own religion is simply outward, it does not behove to collect it.'[155] What he wants to convey is that the Jizia was collected from the non-Muslims, because they did not acknowledge their Muslim ruler as their Spiritual Head in the past, but now as they had acknowledged Akbar as such and their still following the outward practices of their own religion was immaterial, its collection had no justification. Essentially they were not the followers of a different religion. Being aware of the religious beliefs and practices of Akbar during the years following 1564, it is not possible to believe that such an idea could have entered Akbar's head at that time. Even eleven years later, in 1575, as Badauni records, he was issuing orders for the assessment of Jizia upon the Hindus.[156]

The second reason which Abu-l-Fazl gives in favour of the abolition runs, 'The Jizia was collected in the past, because the rulers were poor and in need of money. To-day, when there are thousands of treasures in the Royal Treasury, the Emperor does not need[157] to collect it.'[158] Were there really hoards in the Treasury of Akbar in the beginning of 1564, when his empire comprised less than two provinces?[159] It is unlikely.

Badauni, enumerating the heretic Regulations of Akbar, tells us that the Jizia was abolished in the year 1579.[160] Among the events of the same year Abu-l-Fazl writes that Akbar abolished tha 'Baj' this year and adds that the orders to the same effect were issued earlier too, but they had not proved effective.[161] The orders against the 'Baj' were being issued for the second time. But Abu-l-Fazl does not refer to the abolition of 'Baj' anywhere previous to 1579.

But what was the 'Baj'? When a Muslim ruler attacked some non-Muslim king and the war ended in a peace treaty rather than annexation, the latter had to pay an annual tribute. This tribute has sometime been named as 'Khiraj' and sometime as 'Jizia'. Perhaps a larger tribute was called 'Khiraj' and a smaller one 'Jizia'. Evidently the former from the badly defeated and the latter from a bit stronger opponent. The implied principle might have been that the land of one was legally lost, though he and his subjects had the right of permanent occupation, and the other, along with his people, had simply to pay the price of security from further Muslim attack. Both of these kinds of tribute had the common name of the 'Baj'. Hence the 'Baj' meant Jizia or Khiraj (land revenue plus Jizia) when paid in lump sum by the ruler of a state on behalf of the people of the state.

But did Akbar ever abolish the Baj, the lump sum tributes? Apparently not. Then what sort of imposition did Akbar abolish in 1579? Presumably Baj from individuals *i.e.* Jizia.

Akbar might have issued orders against Jizia in some particular or local instance in 1564; otherwise Nizam-ud-Din Ahmad and Badauni would not have omitted mention of such an important step. Abu-l-Fazl extends the abolition as if of general application,[162] and gives, under the events of 1564, the reasons of its abolition on which it was abolished in 1579.

The use of the word 'Baj' instead of 'Jizya' has created all this trouble. If we put the word Jizia instead and shift the reasons proffered in 1564 to 1579, all the facts drop nearly into place.

If the Baj is Jizia, Abu-l-Fazl refers to the abolition of Jizia previous to 1579 also, under the events of 1564. In 1579 Akbar was really trying to play the part of the Spiritual Head of Hindus and Muslims alike, obliterating distinction between the two.

In 1579 Akbar's treasury was also really full.

In the presence of Badauni's clear statements and after the cross-emamination of Abu-l-Fazl, it is evident that Jizia was not abolished in 1564 as hitherto believed and started in every history book on the period, but in 1579, and that it was not abolished to give them some citizenship[163] which the Hindus under Akbar did not enjoy before its abolition, but as a part of the plan of Akbar's Religious Headship of Hindus and Muslims.

Akbar grew up to be a fervently religious man. With utmost rigour and intensity he worshipped like a Muslim. He searched after the Truth, tried to know the secret of the miraculous powers attributed to prophets and saints, and sought to have a direct communion with God. But in vain. He went from place to place, from religion to religon to see if anywhere there existed what he desired. There was no flash of light to guide him in the darkness. Disappointed, he formulated his own Order. How far it helped him on his path is not known. Perhaps it gave him some consolation at least. But his search continued, with a courage undaunted. Every regulation of his Order may not command our respect, but certainly the man himself does. Those who confessed to follow him might or might not have been sincere in their professions, but he was honest throughout his long journey.

NOTES

1. *Muntakhab,* ii, 274.
2. Attached by the milk ties *i.e.* foster-relation.
3. We may not forget the geographical factor however. Kabul and Bihar-Bengal are wide apart. In those days of slow communications, therefore, in spite of the efforts of the parties concerned, simultaneous action could not be taken. Nobles in Bihar and Bengal rebelled first and invited Mirza Hakim to collaborate with them. Masum Khan Farnakhudi, Governor of Jaunpur and later of Avadh, would not join them until Mirza Hakim had come down and strengthened their cause. By the time the news of Mirza Hakim's invasion reached him and he rose in revolt, rebel leaders in Bihar had already been dispresed. Mirza Hakim was not yet able to create any diversion, when Farnakhudi was attacked and defeated. Next came the turn of

Mirza Hakim to be pursued to the very walls of his capital and be routed there. After Akbar's return from Kabul, rebellion in Bengal was easily suppressed. The rebels had to fight single-handedly and fell one after another.

4. *Akbarnama,* iii, 291.
5. *Akbarnama,* iii, 193.
6. Ibid, 158, 569.
7. *Akbarnama,* iii, 341.
8. The Hill of the Hindu saint Bal Nath. He lived and worshipped there.
9. Jogis: Hindu monks.
10. *Akbarnama,* iii, 350.
11. Ibid, 372.
    Muntakhab, ii, 296.
12. *Muntakhab,* ii, 295-96.
13. *Akbarnama,* iii, 372. تا از این گروه بزرگ دستار دراز آستین آگاه باشد
14. *Akbarnama,* iii, 372.
15. *Muntakhab,* ii, 299.
    Monserrate, cited in *Akbar, The Great Mogul,* V.A. Smith, 176.
16. *Akbarnama,* iii, 309.
17. *Muntakhab,* ii, 299.
18. Mashaikh: saint-like persons.
19. *Muntakhab,* ii, 300.
20. Ibid, 307-8.
21. *i.e.* Islam, Modern compared to the ancient religions of Persians and Hindus.

22-23. *Muntakhab,* ii, 307-8, 256, 262.

24. Ibid, 307, 273, 306.
25. Ibid, 314, 272.
26. Ibid, 322.
27. Ibid, 338-39.
28. *Muntakhab,* ii, 314.
29. و حروفِ خاصه زبانِ عرب مثل ثا و حا و عین و صاد و ضاد و ظا را از تلفظ
    بر طرف ساختند و عبدالله و ابدالله و احدی و اهدی و امثالِ آن اگر می گفتند خوش می‌داشتند
    و آن دو بیتِ شاهنامه را که فردوسی طوسی بطریق نقل آورده متمسک می‌ساختند که
    ز شیر شتر خوردن و سوسمار — عرب را بجائی رسیده است کار
    Muntakhab, ii, 307.
30. *Muntakhab,* ii, 306-7.
    Fiqah: Jurisprudence.
    Tafsir: Commentary on the Quran.
    Hadis: Tradition from the Prophet of Islam.
31. Dajjal: The Anti-Christ.

32. در نهصد و دو قران می‌بینم   و ز مهدی و دجّال نشان می بینم
یا ملک بدل گردد یا گردد دین   سرّی که نهان است عیان می‌بینم

Muntakhab, ii, 313

33. *Muntakhab*, ii, 286-87, 259.
34. Ibid, 326.
35. Abu-l-Fazl, for example, is not ashamed of recording the following story:–

Nine hundred years ago, in the days of Anant Alaail, the ruler of Kashmir, the wine-sellers had got the upper hand and drunkenness and oppression were running rampant. There lived at this time a Brahman named Shivdat in the city of Srinagar. His wife was matchless in beauty and in chastity. He was afraid of the 'hungry glances of the villains, ever turning towards this precious jewel.' He would always seek the protection of the gods against them.

He was advised to consult the spirit, Baital, in this connection. To call in this spirit one had to continue chanting various charms for many a day. When this course was over, he was to carry a human corpse, sound in every limb, to the cremation ground, in the dead of the night, and nail it on the ground, with face downward, at a certain astronomical moment. Then he would sit on its back and light the lamp made of the human skull, with the wick of a piece of the shroud of a dead man and human fat to burn as oil. He was to repeat certain charms and blow on human teeth which were to be sprinkled around like flowers. At this would appear dreadful forms, and if the nerves of the man sitting on the corpse did not give way, the dead body would begin to shake and produce horrible shrieks. After this Baital would appear in a pleasant form and utter the words, 'Why have you taken all this trouble?', and then answer any questions put to him.

Poor Shivdat had to go through all this ordeal. But he was prepared, with the resolution of a lover, to traverse any Hades for his beloved sweet wife.

He had got hold of a dead body for this purpose. But he had still to collect other accessories and was in a fix. Neither could he take it within the city, nor leave it outside without the risk of its being found out or devoured by beasts. Having bound it in a cloth, he carried it to the house of a tanner friend. The stench of the tannery was sure to suppress the foul smell of the rotting corpse. Having entrusted his 'secret' to his friend, Shivdat departed to procure the magic lamp and the magic flowers.

Midnight struck. There appeared Baital and addressed the tanner, "Inform Shivdat. The lease of the oppressors is long. Have patience. have no fear. Twenty men of this line will wear the crown. Then the Kaiths will rule the country. Then the Muslims will come to rule. Then will be the turn of Chaks. When the eighth of them comes to the throne, their rule will come to an end. Then 'the Lord of the Form and the Meaning', whose intentions, whose actions, whose words, will be according to the will of God, will appear to administer justice on the land. Adieu!"

Shivdat related these events in verse for posterity. Today you can read them in ancient manuscripts or engraved on old tablets of stone.

Not a very bad Ghost Story! This is the work of the Kashmiri Pandits. They seem to be particularly interested in the uncanny and the macabre. And Abu-l-Fazl translates its details with the same meticulous care with which he records the organisation of Akbar's cavalry or the Revenue statistics exact to the last hapenny. After all it exalts King Akbar.
(*Akbarnama*, iii, 807-8.)

36. *Muntakhab*, ii, 301.
37. *Akbarnama*, iii, 378 — از انبوهیِ تقلید پیشگانِ خرد دشمن و خرد بلندی گرا شد
38. *Akbarnama*, iii, 378.
    Mutakhab, ii, 301.
39. *Muntakhab*, ii, 256.
40. *Muntakhab*,ii,358 Ibid, 258. — تحقیقِ مذاهب ... حلاوت آن در مذاق افتاده
41. *Muntakhab*, ii, 261.
42. *Akbarnama*, iii, 378.
    Muntakhab, ii, 301.
43, 45, 47. Such significance of these actions is clearly stated in *Muntakhab*. Abu-l-Fazl or Akbar would not dare to.
44. *Muntakhab*, ii, 301, 306.
46. Ibid, 301.
48. Ibid, 306.
    Ain, i, 200.
49. *Ain*, i, 200.
50. Peshkashs: gifts.
51. Vakils: representatives.
52. *Muntakhab*, ii, 287 — و این هم باعثِ دعوای نبوت شد اما نه بلفظ نبوت
53-54. These epithets are not there in exact words, but they are implied in most unequivocal terms.
55. *Muntakhab*, ii, 301, 259.
56. *Ain*, i, 157.

57. Ibid, 157.
58. *Muntakhab,* ii, 308.
59. Ibid, 338.
60. *Muntakhab,* ii, 210. مقصود ما مناسبت لفظی است
61. نعت
62. *Muntakhab,* ii, 269.
63. *Muntakhab,* ii, 325.
64. Ibid, 326.
65. *Akbarnama,* iii, 379-80.
    Muntakhab, ii, 325.
66. *Ain,* i, 160.
67. *Ain,* i, 160.
68. Ain, I, ibo که برو «اسمِ اعظم و طلسمِ اقدس: الله اکبر» نقش کرده‌اند
69. *Ain,* i, 160 شصتِ پاک و نظری پاک خطائی نکند
70. *Ain,* i, 160.
71. *Muntakhab,* ii, 338.
72. Smith, *Akbar, The Great Mogul,* 217-18.
73. *Ain,* i, 160. شصتِ خاصه
74. *Muntakhab,* ii, 338.
75. Ibid, 291.
76. Ibid, 272.
77. *Muntakhab,* ii, 304-5.
78. Ibid, 260.
79. Ibid, 404.
80. Ibid, 261.
81. Ibid, 341.
82. Ibid, 260.
83. Ibid, 260.
84. *Muntakhab,* ii, 261.
85. Ibid, 322.
86. Ibid, 322.
87. Ibid, 321-22.
88. *Ain,* i, 159.
89. *Muntakhab,* ii, 357.
90. Ibid, 356-57.
91. *Muntakhab,* ii, 340-41.
92. Ibid, 391.
93. Ibid, 351.
94. Ibid, 391.
95. Ibid, 261.
96. *Akbarnama,* iii, 524, 529, 569, 826, 837.
    Khusrau (b.1587), son of Prince Salim.

Rustam (b. 1588), son of Prince Murad.
Parvez (b. 1589), son of Prince Salim.
Khurram (b. 1591), son of Prince Salim.
His name is also Persian, though not of the Chosroes.
Hoshang (b. 1604), son of Prince Danyal.
Tahmuras, son of Prince Danyal.

97. *Muntakhab,* ii, 325-26.
98. Ibid, 326.
99. *Muntakhab,* ii, 273.
100. Ibid, 325.
101. Ibid, 303.
102. *Muntakhab,* ii, 303, 375-76.
103. Ibid, 306.
104. Ibid, 322.
105. Ibid, 321-22.
Ain, i, 59.
106. *Ain,* i, 161.
107. *Muntakhab,* ii, 322.
108. Smith, *Akbar, The Great Mogul, 166.*
109. *Ain,* i, 161.
Muntakhab, ii, 322.
110. *Muntakhab,* ii, 303.
111. *Akbarnama,* iii, 771, 831.
112. Muftis: jurists.
113. *Muntakhab,* ii, 306.
114. Ibid, 261, 322.
115. As Christians relapsed into the pagan practice of image-worship. They ceased to worship God without bowing before the image of Christ on the Cross, or that of the Holy Virgin with the Child, actually the portrait of some model wrapped in red and blue—might be of some mistress of a Raphael with her child really born before marriage.
116. *Ain,* i, 117.
117. *Akbarnama,* iii, 596.
118. *Muntakhab,* ii, 261-62.
119. *Akbarnama,* iii, 626, 647.
120. *Muntakhab,* ii, 324-25.
121. *Ain,* i, 161.
Muntakhab, ii, 305-6.
122. *Muntakhab,* ii, 338.
Ain, i, 196-97.
123. *Muntakhab,* ii, 356.

124. Actually in the form of human body with four hands and the head of a wild boar—one of the 'Avatars' of Vishnu who is one of the Hindu Triad, the 'Trimurti': Brahma the Creator, Vishnu the Preserver and Shiva the Destroyer (and Regenerator).
125. *Muntakhab,* ii, 305.
126. *Muntakhab,* ii, 376.
Ain, i, 161.
127. *Muntakhab,* ii, 356.
128. Ibid, 304, 338.
129. *Muntakhab,* ii, 306.
Ain, i, 201.
130. *Muntakhab,* ii, 356.
131. Ibid, 391.
132. *Ain,* i, 161.
133. *Muntakhab,* ii, 376.
134. *Muntakhab,* ii, 305.
135. *Muntakhab,* ii, 391-2.
136. Ibid, 356.
Ain, i, 201.
137. *Muntakhab,* ii, 338-39.
Ain, i, 201.
138. *Muntakhab,* ii, 356.
139. *Muntakhab,* ii, 376.
140. Ibid, 356.
141. Ibid, 306-7, 363.
142. Ibid, 391.
143. Ibid, 356.
144. Ibid, 391
145. Ibid, 392.
146. Ibid, 391.
147. *Muntakhab,* ii, 338.
148. Ibid, 302.
149. Ibid, 391.
150. Ibid, 303.
151. *Muntakhab,* ii, 301.
152. در دورِ پادشاهِ خطابخش و جرم پوش قاضی قرابه کش شد و مفتی پیاله نوش
Ibid, 309.
Akbarnama, iii, 582.
153. The trouble in the way of appreciating Muslim History is that it has not yet become the history of a people of the past, which does not touch our feelings and sentiments. Till yesterday the Sick Man of Europe was a factor in international politics. Even

in his sickness he would set the Austrian Eagles, Russian Bears and British Lions one against the other with such a deftness of hand that it is impossible not to praise the rogue. Such was Sultan Abdul Hamid II whom Europeans in impotent rage would call 'Abdul the Damned', 'the Venomous Reptile' and the like. The last Muslim hero, Usman Nuri Pasha, the Defender of Pelvena, is not yet forgotten. And the last Muslim victor is alive to-day—Asmat Anonu, who defeated the Greecks on the battle-field near the village of Anonu, though they were well supported by the 'Determined Bulldogs' and the 'Welsh Wolves'. And Muslims may still create trouble on the banks of the Suez Canal, or on the oil-fields of Iran.

154. How Muslims too came to pay Khiraj may be explained. Muslims had to pay a levy called 'ushr' on land produce. It was a tax, one tenth of the produce, while 'Khiraj' was a rental, one fourth or a bit more of the produce.

When big cities sprang up under the Muslim rule, giving rise to industries and trade and demand for labour, it became profitable for the Khiraji tillers of land to leave the plough and come to the cities. The Muslims were pleased to buy their lands. But they were not particularly interested in agriculture. Moreover, they would pay only 'ushr' instead of the 'Khiraj'. The Khiraji tillers of land began to migrate to cities. The whole economic structure seemed to break down.

Hajjaj, the famous Viceroy of the East–Mesopotamia, Persia, Turkistan and Sind—dealt with the situation in his characteristic ruthless, though efficient manner. He declared that no tiller of land could leave his land. Severe punishments were enforced. Many of them were branded, so that no story could help them if they broke the law.

Later the Doctors of Law gave a ruling, safeguarding the state against the loss of revenue. According to it the Khiraji lands remained Khiraji even after passing into the hands of Muslims. The Muslim holders had to pay Khiraj and not 'ushr' for these lands. The underlying principle seems to be that the original non-Muslim holders had no proprietary rights. They had only holding rights. The new Muslim occupants had, therefore, purchased rights of holding land, not the land itself, which was still the property of the state. Hence they had to pay the rental and not the tax. Thus after some time most of the land in Muslim hands was also Khiraji. In later centuries, as under the Mughuls in India, the differentiation disappeared and the Muslim holders of land had to pay the same amount of land revenue as non-Muslims.

But when the state collected Khiraj from the Muslims, they were being regularly paid, in cash or in jagirs, for the military service, while in the days of receiving lands on which they paid 'ushr', they formed the national forces which were not paid by the state.

155. *Akbarnama,* ii, 203.
156. امروز .... آنانکه در کیشِ دیگراند چون یکجهتان یک دین از ته دل کمرِ خدمت و «عقیدت» بر میانِ جان بسته در ارتقاء مدارج علیای دولت اهتمام دارند چگونه «این اصحابِ تباین را که اساسِ آن بمحض تقلید است» و «ارادت و عقیدت در آنها نقد» بر آن گروه سابق که عداوتِ جانی در میان بود قیاس نموده ... آید

     Akbarnama, ii, 204.
157. *Muntakhab,* ii, 210.
158. Certainly Akbar who collected land revenue at the rate of a little more than one third of the produce did not need the collection of Jizia. Had he limited himself to Islamic taxation, he would have surely needed it.
159. و نیز باعث عمده بر اخذ این وجه در زمان پیش فرط احتیاج منتظمان و معاونان بمصالح و اسباب دنیوی بوده تا بدین روش وسعتی در معاش پدید آید. امروز که هزاران گنج در خزینه انتظام بخش جهان پدید است ـ چگونه منصف دانای ممیز دل بر گرفتنِ این مال نهد.

     Akbarnama, ii, 204.
160. The Punjab and most of the parts of the present U.P.
161. *Muntakhab,* ii, 276.
162. *Akbarnama,* iii, 295-96.
163. And where Abu-l-Fazl has not done this, others have proved his equals. In every history book it is stated that Akbar in 1563 abolished the Pilgrimage Tax in his Empire and gave Freedom of Worship to the Hindus. Actually, in 1563, soon after his marriage with the Rajput princess of Amber, Akbar abolished at only one place the tax collected at the time of pilgrimage and fair. (*Akbarnama*, ii, 190). Happily at this time, when the empire of Akbar consisted of less than two provinces, there was only this one important place of Hindu pilgrimage (Mathura). Hence some ground for the generalisation. But It has yet to be decided whether this tax was a Religious Persecution Tax or a tax levied on economic basis, because at the time of pilgrimage there used to be held a fair with its brisk market.
164. Sri Ram Sharma, *The Religious Policy of the Mughal Emperors,* 23.

Appendix B

Muslims and Hindus in Akbar's service

Muslims and Hindus under Akbar were put on various services together. Their names give an insight into the period.

1573

In the second Gujarat expedition, in 1573, those who accompanied Akbar were Mirza Khan, Saif Khan Kuka, Zain Khan Kuka, Husain Khan Tukriya, Abd-Allah Khan, *Jagan Nath*[1], *Rai Sal, Jai Mal, Jagmal Patvar,* Khwaja Ghias-ud-Din Ali Asif Khan, *Raja Birbar, Raja Dip Chand,* Mir Ghias-ud-din Ali Naqib Khan, Muhammad Zaman, Bahadur Khan, *Man Singh Darbari,*Sayyid Khwaja, Shaikh Abd-ur-Rahim, *Ram Das Kachhwaha, Ram Chand,* Bahadur Khan Quradar, *Sanwal Das, Jadun Kaisth Darbari,* Surkh Badakhshi, *Duvar Bhalla, Har Das, Tara Chand Khwas and Lal Kalavant.*

In the same campaign among the emperor's personal guards there were the musketeers *Salbahan,* Qadar Quli and *Ranjit.*

A iii 49, 51[2]

1574

Next year when Akbar proceeded towards Bihar, where imperial forces were fighting against the Afghans under their king, Davud, he was accompanied by *Raja Bhagwan Das, Raja Man Singh,* Zain Khan Kuka, Shahbaz Khan, Sadiq Khan, Qasim Khan Mir-i-Bahr, *Raja Birbar,* Jalal Khan, Mirzada Ali Khan, Sayyid Abd-Allah Khan, *Madhav Singh,* Naqib Khan, Qamar Khan, Mir Sharif and Niyabat Khan.

And travelling together down the Ganges in a boat there were Qazi-i-Askar, *Bhagwan Das Khazanchi* and Sher Beg.

A iii 87,94

1580

During the campaign against the Bengal-Bihar rebels, in one of the battles the centre was commanded by Tarsun Khan, *Raja Todar Mal, Rai Surjan, Raja Askarn* and Mihtar Khan.

A iii 307

1581

When Kabul was invaded by the Mughuls under prince Murad in 1581, he was accompanied at the centre by Mirza Yusuf Khan, *Rai Rai Singh, Rai Durga,* Gujar Khan, *Suraj Singh, Madan Chauhan,* Shaikh Abd-ur-Rahim, *Balka Rai, Ram Chand, Thakursi,* Salim Khan, Kakar Ali, Sayyid Muhammad Mauji, Karam-Allah Kambo, *Prithvi Raj, Ram Das Chauhan, Mathura Das, Sanwal Das, Kalla Kachhwaha, Askarn, Kajra,* Hazara Beg, Shaikh Wali Jalal and Mir Muhsin.

And the vanguard was commanded by *Raja Man Singh,* Naurang Khan, Sheruya Khan, *Madhav Singh,* Muhammad Beg Tuklu, *Man Singh Dalbari, Jagmal Salahdar,* Bahadur Khan Quadar, *Surjan,* Pahlavan Ali, *Sakat Singh, Jagat Rai, Ram Chand, Bhagwan Das,* Shaikh Kabir, Jabbar Quli and Naqib Divana.

A iii 353

1583

When Muzaffar Shah attacked the Imperialists in Gujarat, a strong force under Mirza Khan was despatched at once. Among his companions there were Sayyid Qasim, Sayyid Hashim, Sheruya Khan, *Rai Durga, Rai Lunkarn, Medni Rai,* Mian Bahadur, Darvish Khan, Raafe Sarmadi, Shaikh Kabir and Nasib Turkman.

In the ensuing battle of Sarkhej, in which Muzaffar was defeated, one of the wings was commanded by *Mota Raja, Rai Durga, Tulsi Das Jadun, Bija Devra* and *Rai Narayan Das.*

And the vanguard was under Painda Khan Mughul, Sayyid Hashim, *Rai Lunkarn, Ram Chand, Udai Singh,* Sayyid Bhadur, Sayyid Shah Ali, Sayyid Nasr-Allah and Sayyid Karam-Allah.

In another division there were *Medni Rai, Ramsah, Raja Mukutman,* Khwaja Raafe, Mukammal Beg Sarmadi, Nasib Turkman, Daulat Khan Lodi, Said Khan Karrani, Shaikh Wali, Shaikh Zain and Khizr Aqa. *A* iii 413,424

1584

To punish Sayyid Daulat in Cambay were sent *Mota Raja, Medni Rai, Raja Mukutman, Ramsah, Udai Singh, Ram Chand, Bagh Rathor, Tulsi Das Jadun,* Daulat Khan Lodi, Bahadur Anul Gakkhar, Abu-l-Fath Mughul and Qara Bahri. *A* iii 436-37

1585

In an action against Muzaffar Shah of Gujarat, in 1585, Khan-khanan's vanguard was under *Madan Chauhan, Ram Chand, Udai Singh,* Sayyid Lad, Sayyid Bahadur, Sayyid Shah Ali, *Keshav Das Rathor, Bhupat Dakkhni,* and *Bhag Rathor.*

When Khan-i-Azam was sent to Malwa to make preparations for the Deccan invasion, those who were ordered to accompany him included Abd-ul-Muttalib Khan, *Raja Askarn,* Sheruya Khan, Mir Jamal-ud-Din Hussain Anju, Burhan-ul-Mulk Dakkhni, Abd-ur-Rahman Muid Beg, Haji Abd-Allah Kashghari, Sulaiman Quli Turk, Ali Murad, Sher Muhammad, Ali Quli, Shihab-ud-Din Ahmad Khan, *Mudhukar, Jagman, Krishn Das,* Asaf Khan, Khwajagi Fath-Allah and Mukhtar Beg.

A iii 464-65

1586

In 1586 Zain Khan Kuka was commissioned against the Afghan tribes in Bajaur and Swat and those who accompanied him included Arab Khanjahani, Hasan Khan Pattni, *Raja Mukutman,* Janash Bahadur, *Askarn, Panchatan, Hira Pardhan, Ram Chand,* Shaikh Kabir, Faulad, Muhammad Ali Saldoz, *Raghu Nath Sashodhiya, Sunar Chand,* Khan Muhammad, Shaikh Maruf, Khanzada Muhammad Padshah Quli, Daulat Baloch, Muhammad Said, Yar Muhammad, Mir Tufan, Rahmat-Allah, Alam Yadgar, Mulla Sheri, Hasan Beg Gurd, Allahbakhsh Murl and Shah Muhammad Isa. *A* iii 475

1590

When Akbar intended to invade Qandhar and an army was mobilized under Khan-khanan, it included Khwaja Muqim, Shah Beg Khan, Sayyid Baha-ud-Din, Bakhtyar Beg, *Govardhan, Raval Bhim, Dalpat,* Janash Bahadur, Bahadur Khan Qurdar,

Muhammad Khan Niyazi, Ali Mardan Bahadur, *Ballabhdhar Rathor,* Sher Khan, Qara Beg, Faridun Birlas Sarmadi, Mir Masum Bhakkri, Hassan Ali Arab, Khwaja Hassam-ud-Din, Sayyid Darvish, Qasim Kuka, Khaki Gallahban, Nur Muhammad, Khwaja Khizri, Abd-ul-Ghani, Ulugh Beg, Khaki Beg, Sayyid Mir Ali, Mirza Beg, Salar Quli, Mirza Muhammad, Sayyid Bandah Ali, Ibrahim Beg, Murshid Quli Jolak, Shamsher-i-Arab, Muhammad Zaman, Baqi Chahardangi, Abd-ul-Latif, Bahadaur Mulk, Izzat Ali Kabuli, Allahbardi Tulakchi, Ilyas Topchi, Muhammad Quli Tingribardi, Farrukh Beg and Qul Muhammad. *A* iii 584-85

1591

In 1591 Prince Murad was appointed Governor of Malwa to organise an offensive against the Deccan Sultanates and those who were ordered to accompany him included Ismail Quli Khan, Mukhtar Beg, *Jagan Nath, Rai Durga,* Abd-Allah Khan, Haji Sainduk, Riza Quli, Mirza Khan, Qabil Beg, Qasim Beg Tabrizi, Qasim Beg Zulqadr, Mahmud Khan, Atam Bahadur, Sidi Rihan, Zia-ud-Din Yusuf, Alam Khan, Naqib Divana, Shaikh Maruf, Mirza Muhammad, Shaikh Abd-Allah, Bakhtyar Said, Mir Kalan Kolabi, *Rai Singh,* Afzal Tulakchi, *Bhupat,* Arif Imad, Abd-ur-Rahim, Lal Beg, Amir Beg, Anfas Beg, Qaya Beg, *Kalyan Das Kochak,* Zaman Beg, Muhammad Wis Kolabi, Bayazid, Imam Quli, Sultan Mahmud, Muhammad Atam, Mahmud Beg, *Ranjit, Ishar Das,* Amir Qaraval, Khwaja Mubarak, *Banvari Das,* Wafadar, Hasan Beg, Muhammad Beg Turkman, *Niramsal, Sazdosal* and *Lakshmi Das.* *A* iii 599-600

1592

Under *Man Singh* against the Afghans in Orissa were fighting Tulak Khan, Farrukh Khan, Ghazi Khan Maidani, Mir Qasim Badakhshi, *Rai Bhoj, Sangram Singh, Akbar Panchatan, Chandra Sen, Bhupat Singh,* Barkhurdar, *Madhav, Lakhi Rai Kokra, Puran Mal Kedhoria, Rup Narayan Sashodhiya,* Yusuf Khan, Makhsus Khan, Bahadur Khan, Tahir Khan, *Babu Mankli,* Khwaja Baqir Ansari, Makhdumzada, Mirza Muhammad Divana, Pahar Khan, Baqir Khan, *Durjan Singh, Subhan Singh,*

Subl Singh, Nuram Kuka, Shihab-ud-Din, sons of Ulugh Khan Habashi, Muzaffar and Khwajagi Inayat-Allah. *A* iii 611

To attack Raja Ram Chand, *Man Singh* sent Mir Sharif Sarmadi, Mir Qasim Badakhshi, Barkhurdar, Abu-l-Baqa, Mahmud Beg Shamlu and Shihab-ud-Din Divana under *Jagat Singh.* *A* iii 631

1593

Akbar married his daughter Shakkar-un-Nisa Begum to Mirza Shahrukh and he was appointed Governor of Malwa. He proceeded to his charge accompanied by Shahbaz Khan, Haidar Dost, Saif-Allah, *Durjan Kachhwaha, Ram Chand Chauhan, Kalla Rathor,* Maqsud Mir-i-Aab, Fath-Allah Kambo, Muhammad Zaman, *Narhar Das,* Salih, Ali Dost, Mir Fazl, Yar Muhammad Qurdar, *Rana Sanga,* Dost Muhammad and *Suraj Mal.* *A*iii 644

1596

When Khan-khanan and Mirza Shahrukh under Prince Murad marched against the combined forces of the three sultanates of the Deccan, the Imperial vanguard was under *Jagan Nath, Rai Durga, Raj Singh, Ram Chand, Keshav Das, Sanwal Das, Raghu Mal, Bhim Narayan Das, Manohar, Prithvi Raj, Narhar Das,* Kaivankulah, *Sakat Singh,* Sultan Bhatti, *Thakursi, Bhoj Raj, Paras Ram* and Shaikh Jamal. *A* iii 718

1600

Asir had fallen and Akbar was subduing the neighbouring country. Abu-l-Fazl was sent towards Nasik accompanied by *Rai Rai Singh, Rai Durga, Rai Bhoj,* Hashim Beg Tulak, Muqim Beg, Faulad Khan and Kamil-ud-Mulk. *A* iii 784

Throughout his rule Akbar's forces were composed of Muslims and Hindus. Muslims of all descriptions, of various races and various countries: Turks, Mongols, Afghans, Arabs, Habashis, Iranis, Hindis–Birlas, Saldoz, Tuklu, Shamlu, Tulak, Anju, Turkman, Kashghari, Badakhshi, Kolabi, Maidani, Kabuli, Karrani, Lodi, Niyazi, Ansari, Tabrizi, Gakkhar, Murl, Kambo, Baloch, Bhakkri, Dakkhni, Mirzas, Khans, Sayyids, Khwajas,

Shaikhs, and Hindus of all denominations: Kachhwahas, Rathors, Chauhans, Sashodhiyas, Kshatris, Kaidhorias, Kaisths, Patvars were all welded together to form one single block—the Akbarian force.

---

1. In italics: names of Hindu officials.
2. A iii 49 = *Akbarnama*, iii, 49.

Appendix C

Akbar's Hindu Mansabdars

Haft Hazari

Raja Man Singh

Panj Hazari

Raja Bhar Mal
Raja Bhagwan Das
Jagan Nath
Bikrmajit

Chahar Hazari

Raja Todar Mal
Raja Rai Singh

Sih Hazari

Madhav Singh
Raj Singh
Rai Pitr Das

Do Hazar Panj Sadi

Rai Sal Darbari

Do Hazari

Raja Kalyan Mal
Raja Lunkarn
Rai Surjan
Raja Gopal
Raja Ram Chand Bhughela
Khankar
Ram Das Kachhwaha
Bhao Singh
Maha Singh
Birbar

Yak Hazar Panj Sadi

Raja Udai Singh
Rai Durga Sashodhiya
Rupsi
Jagat Singh

Yak Hazari

Askarn
Jagmal
Pratap Singh
Sakat Singh
Medni Rai Chauhan
Kalyan Das
Rai Bhoj
Raja Syam Singh
Raja Jagman Chauhan

Haft Sadi

Salhadi
Dharu

Panj Sadi

Raval Bhim
Durjan Singh
Sahal Singh
Dalpat
Jagmal Patvar
Parmanand Kshatri
Ram Chand Bundela
Raja Mukutman Bhedoria
Raja Ram Chand of Orissa

Chahar Sadi

Rai Manohar
Ram Chand Kachhwaha
Balka

Sih Sadi

Ballabhdhar Rathor
Keshav Das
Tulsi Das Jadun
Man Singh Kachhwaha
Krishna Das

Do Sadi

Rai Ram Das Diwan
Jagat Singh
Mathura Das Kshatri
Sanwal Das Jadun
Udand of Orissa
Keshav Das Rathor
Suthra Das
Sanga Patvar
Sunder of Orissa
Sakra
Kalla Kachhwaha
Lala

There must have been other Hindu mansabdars also, but unfortunately their mansabs are not recorded anywhere.

Appendix D

Hindus in Akbar's service

Acting Vakil-i-Saltanat
Raja Todar Mal
Chief Diwans
Raja Todar Mal
Rai Pitr Das
Diwans at the Centre
Raja Todar Mal
Rai Pitr Das
Prominent Commanders
Raja Bhagwan Das
Raja Man singh
Raja Todar Mal
Rai Rai Singh
Raja Udai Singh
Jagan Nath
Askarn
Lunkarn
Ram Chand
Rai Durga
Rai Surjan
Rai Sal
Madhav Singh
Rai-rayan Bikrmajit
Provincial Governors
Raja Bhagwan Das
Raja Man Singh
Raja Todar Mal
Rai Rai Singh

Joint Provincial Governors
Jagan Nath
Askarn
Rai Durga
Officiating Diwan at the Centre
Rai Ram Das
Duputy Diwans at the Centre
Rai Pitr Das
Rai Ram Das
Assistant Diwan at the Centre
Madhav Singh
In the Central Government
Jagan Nath
Askarn
Jagmal
Rai Durga
Rai Surjan
Rai Sal
Provincial Bakhshis
Rai Purushottam
Tara Chand
Provincial Diwans
Krishna Das
Ram Das
Bharati Chand
Rai Ram Das
Khanur
Mathura Das
Ram Rai
Keshav Das

Appendix E

The House of Amber in the service of Akbar

Raja Bhar Mal of Amber, holding the Rank of the Commandant of 5,000 cavalry.

Raja Bhagwan Das,	5,000,	son of Bhar Mal.
Raja Man Singh,	7,000,	son of Bhagwan Das.
Askarn,	1,000,	brother of Bhar Mal.
Jagmal,	1,000,	brother of Bhar Mal.
Rupsi,	1,500,	brother of Bhar Mal.
Jagan Nath,	5,000,	son of the Bhar Mal.
Salhadi,	700,	son of Bhar Mal.
Madhav Singh,	3,000,	son of Bhagwan Das.
Pratap Singh,	1,000,	son of Bhagwan Das.
Raj Singh,	3,000,	son of Askarn.
Khankar,	2,000,	son of Jagmal.
Jagat Singh,	1,500,	son of Man Singh.
Sakat Singh,	1,000,	son of Man Singh.
Bhao Singh,	2,000,	son of Man Singh.
Durjan Singh,	500,	son of Man Singh.
Sahal Singh,	500,	son of Man Singh.
Jagat Singh,	200,	son of Man Singh.
Maha Singh,	2,000,	son of Jagat Singh, 1,500.
Himmat Singh,	....	son of Man Singh.
Chandr Bhan,	....	brother of Man Singh.
Suraj Singh,	....	brother of Man Singh.
Jai Mal,	....	son of Rupsi.

Raja Bhar Mal, his 3 brothers, 3 sons, 3 nephews, 5 grandsons, 7 great-grandsons and 1 great-great-grandson.

Bibliography

1. Important Contemporary Authorities

Abd-ul-Qadir Badauni, *Muntakhab-ut-Tawarikh*, Vols.ii and iii, Bibliotheca Indica, Calcutta, 1865 and 1869.

Abd-l-Fazl, *Akbarnama*, Vols, ii and iii, Bibliotheca Indica, Calcutta, 1879 and 1886.

Abu-l-Fazl, *Ain-i-Akbari*, Vol. i, Bibiliotheca Indica, Calcutta, 1872.

Nizam-ud-Din Ahmad, *Tabaqat-i-Akbar*,Vol. ii, Bibliotheca Indica, Calcutta, 1931.

2. Other Contemporary Works

Abd-ul- Haq, *Tarikh-i-Haqqi*, MSS.

Asad Beg, *Waqiat-i-Asad Beg*, Elliot and Dawson, Vol. iv, pp. 150-74.

Qandhari, *Tarikh-i-Muhammad Arif Qandhari*.

Maulana Ahmad and others, *Tarikh-i-Alifi*, Elliot and Dowson, Vol. v, pp. 167-76.

Muhammad Qasim Frishta, *Tarikh-i-Frishta*, Bombay, 1832.

Nur-ud-Din Muhammad Jahangir Padshah Ghazi, *Tuzk-i-Jahangiri*, Aligarh, 1864.

Monserrate, A., *Mongolicae Legationis Commentarius*, English translation by J.S. Hoyland, London, 1922.

Pierre Du Jarric, *Akbar and the Jesuits*, Translated by C.H. Payne, Routledge, London, 1926.

Fitch, R., *England's Pioneer to India*, ed. J.H. Riley, London, 1899.

Early Travels in India, ed. W. Foster, 1921.

3. Modern Works

Sharma, Sri Ram, *Religious Policy of the Mughal Emperors*, Oxford, 1940.

Roychoudhury, M. L., *The Din-i-Ilahi*, Calcutta, 1941.

Kennedy, Vans, *Some Notices respecting the Religion introduced by Akbar,* Translations of the Literary Society of Bombay, Vol. ii, Chapter XI, pp. 242-270, London, 1820.

Wilson, H.H., *Account of the Religious Innovations attempted by Akbar,* Quarterly Oriental Magazine, Vol. i, pp. 49-62, Calcutta, 1824.

Blochmann, H. *Badauni and his Works,* Journal of the Asiatic Society of Bengal, No. i, pp. 105-144, 1869.

Modi, J.J., *The Parsees at the Court of Akbar,* Bombay, 1903.

Goldie, F., *The First Christian Mission to the Great Mogul,* Dublin, 1897.

Maclagan, E.D., *The Jesuit Missions to the Emperor Akbar,* journal of the Asiatic Society of Bengal, i, Vol. lxv, 1896.

Smith, V. A., *Akbar, The Great Mogul,* Clarendon Press, 1919.

Von Noir, Count, *The Emperor Akbar,* Translated by A. Beveridge, Calcutta, 1890.

Binyon, L., *Akbar,* London, 1932.

Muhammad Husain Azad, *Darbar-i-Akbari* (in Urdu), Lahore, 1921.

Combridge History of India, Vol. iv, 1937.

Sharma, S.R., *The Mughal Empire in India, 1526-1761,* Bombay, 1934.

Tripathi, R.P., *Rise and Fall of the Mughal Empire,* Allahabad, 1959.

Ibn Hasan, *The Central Structure of the Mughal Empire,* London, 1936.

Saran, P., *The Provincial Government of the Mughals,* Allahabad, 1941.

Sharma, Sri Ram, *Mughal Government and Administration,* Bombay 1951.

Qureshi, Ishtiaq Husain, *The Administration of the Mughal Empire,* Karachi, 1966.

Binyon and Arnold, *The Court Painters of the Grand Moguls,* London, 1921.

Brown, P., *Indian Painting under the Mughals,* Oxford, 1924.

Index